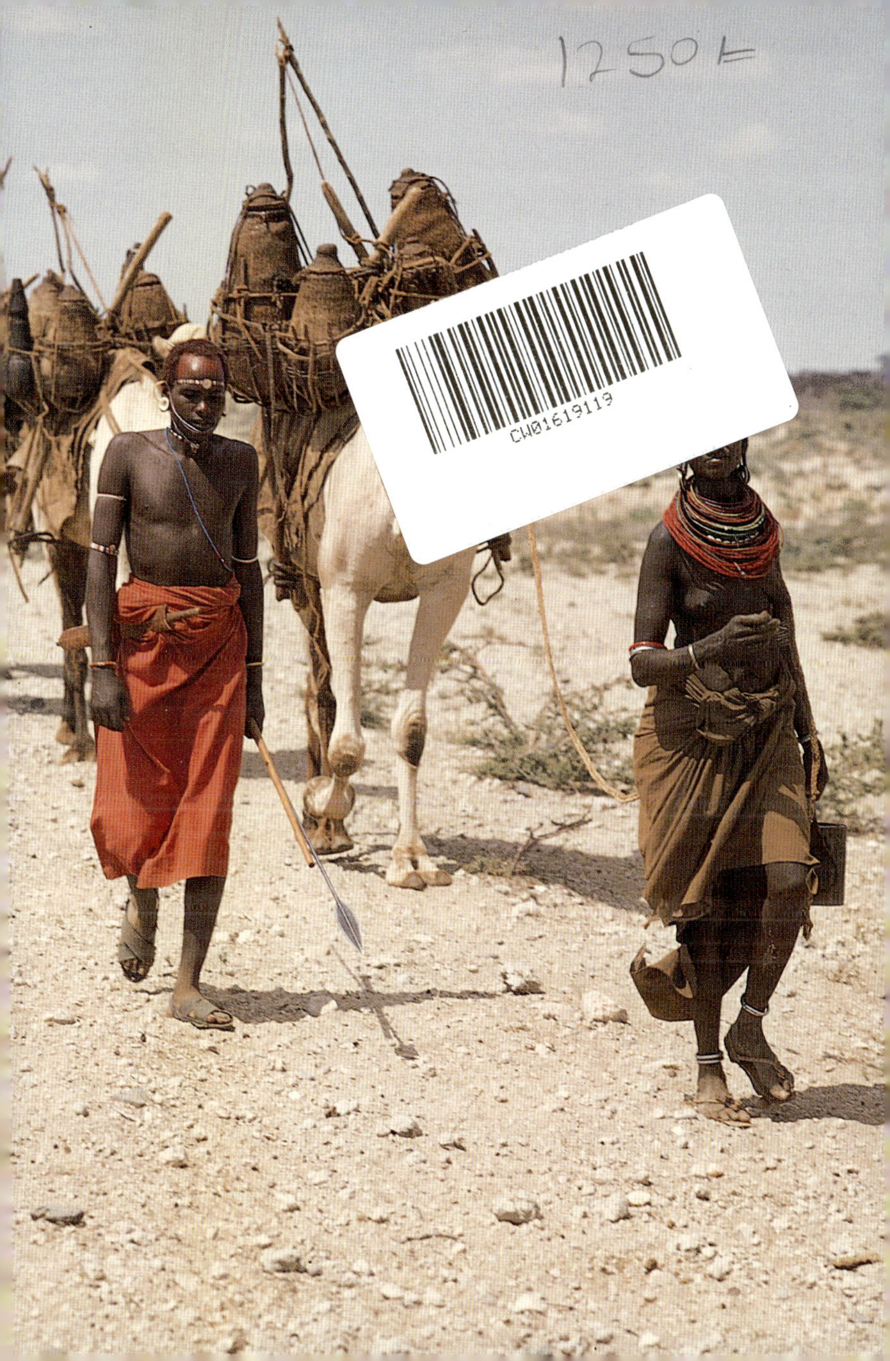

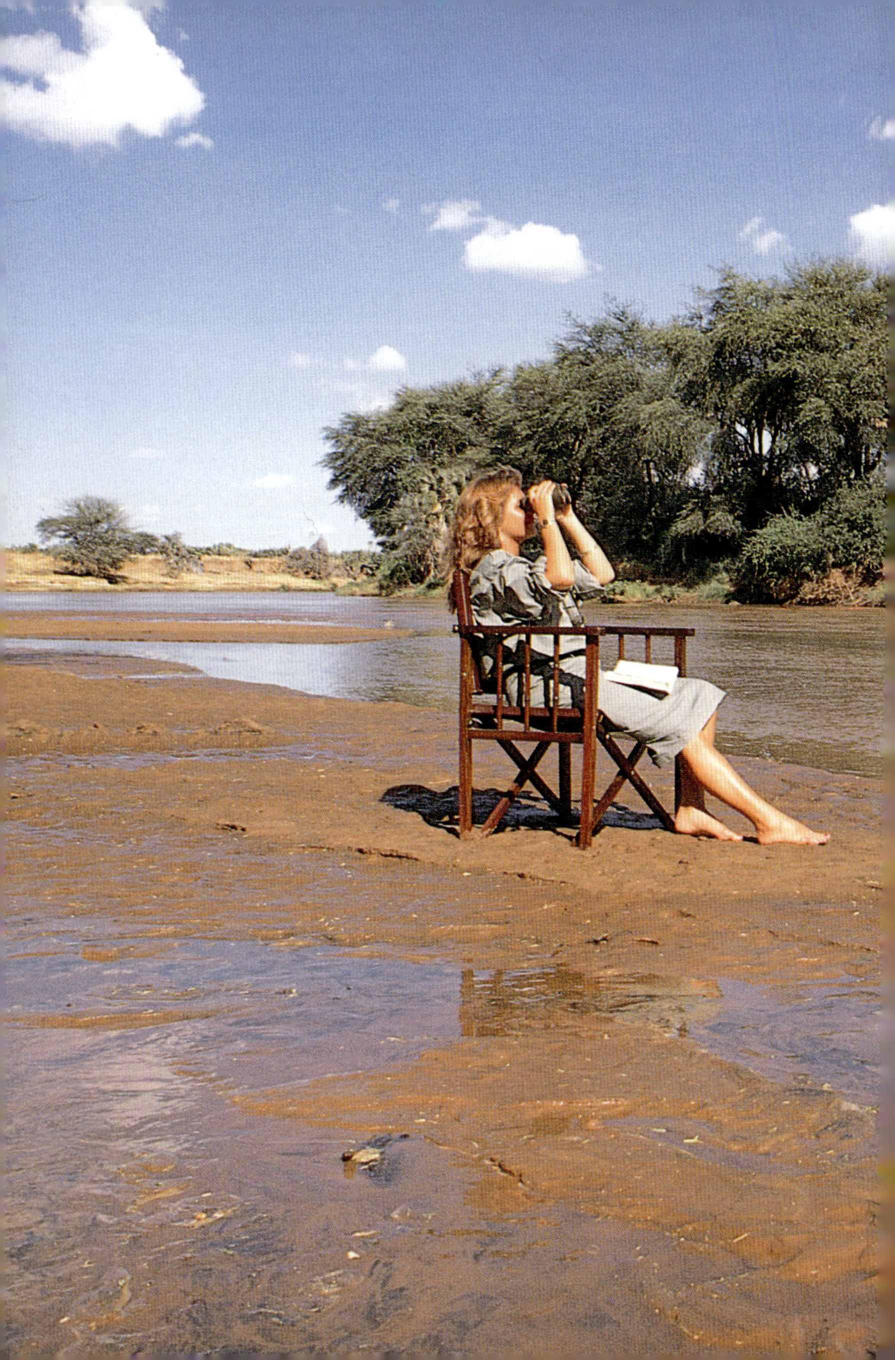

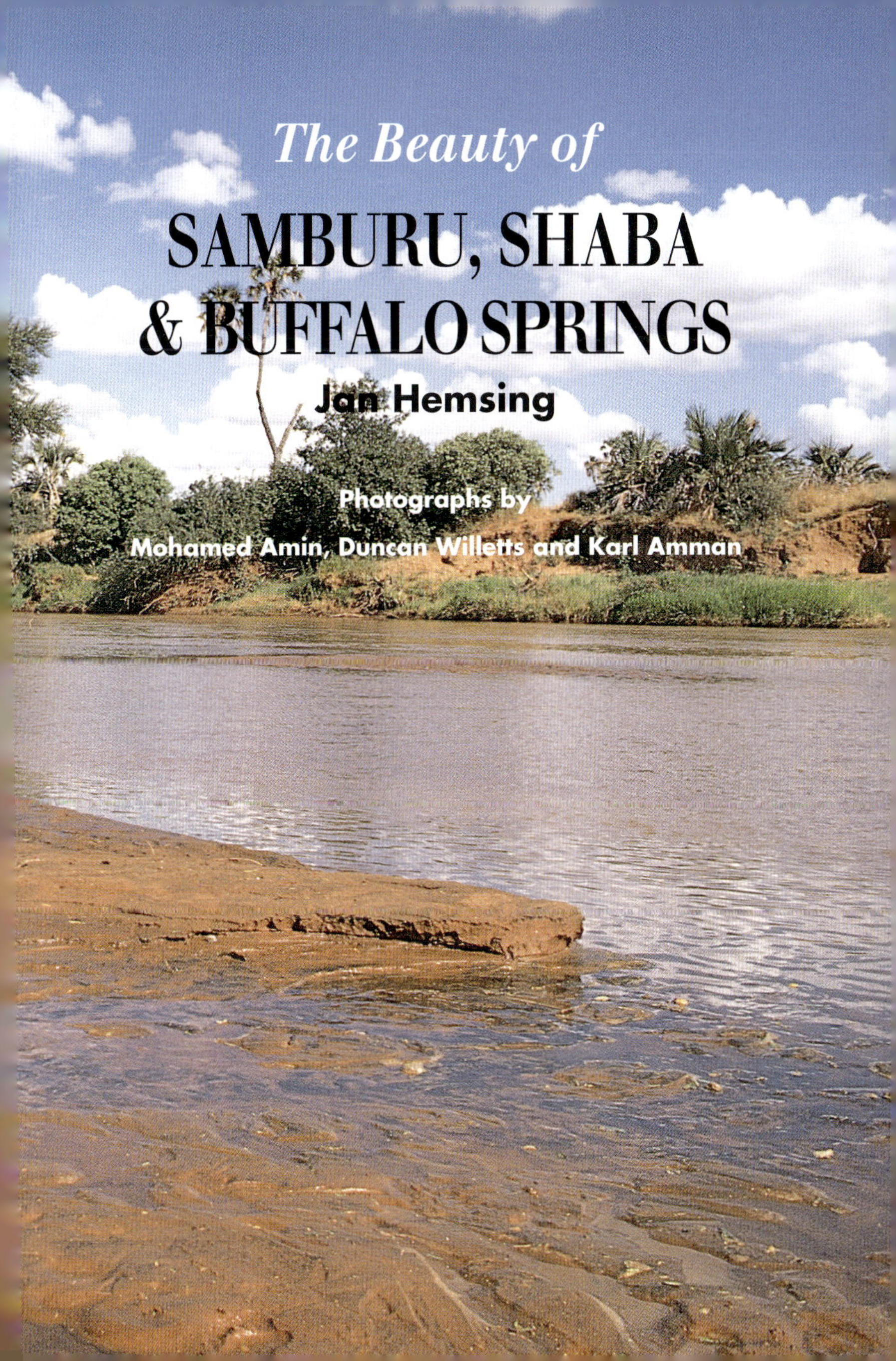

The Beauty of

SAMBURU, SHABA & BUFFALO SPRINGS

Jan Hemsing

Photographs by

Mohamed Amin, Duncan Willetts and Karl Amman

First published in 1997 by
Cameraрix Publishers International
PO Box 45048
Nairobi, Kenya

ISBN 1 874041 28 8

This book was designed and produced by
Camerapix Publishers International
PO Box 45048
Nairobi, Kenya

Edited by Brian Tetley

Half title: Moving day in Samburuland.
Title page: The wide brown Uaso Nyiro River.
Contents page: Little bee-eaters.
*Overleaf: Grevy's zebra (*Equus grevyi*)*

Printed in Singapore by Tien Wah Press

Contents

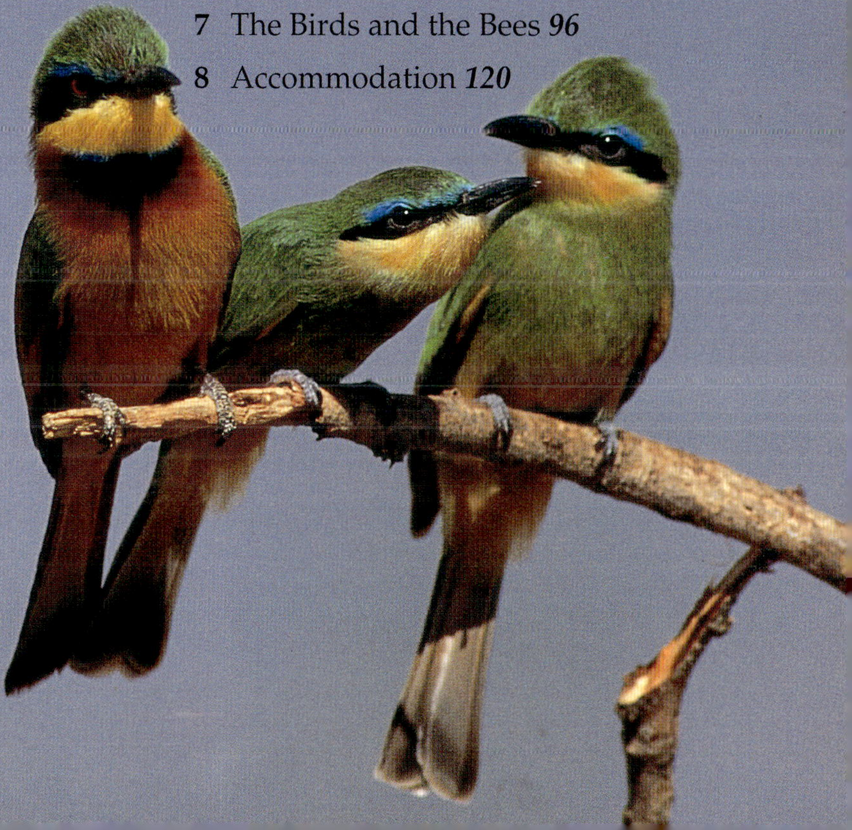

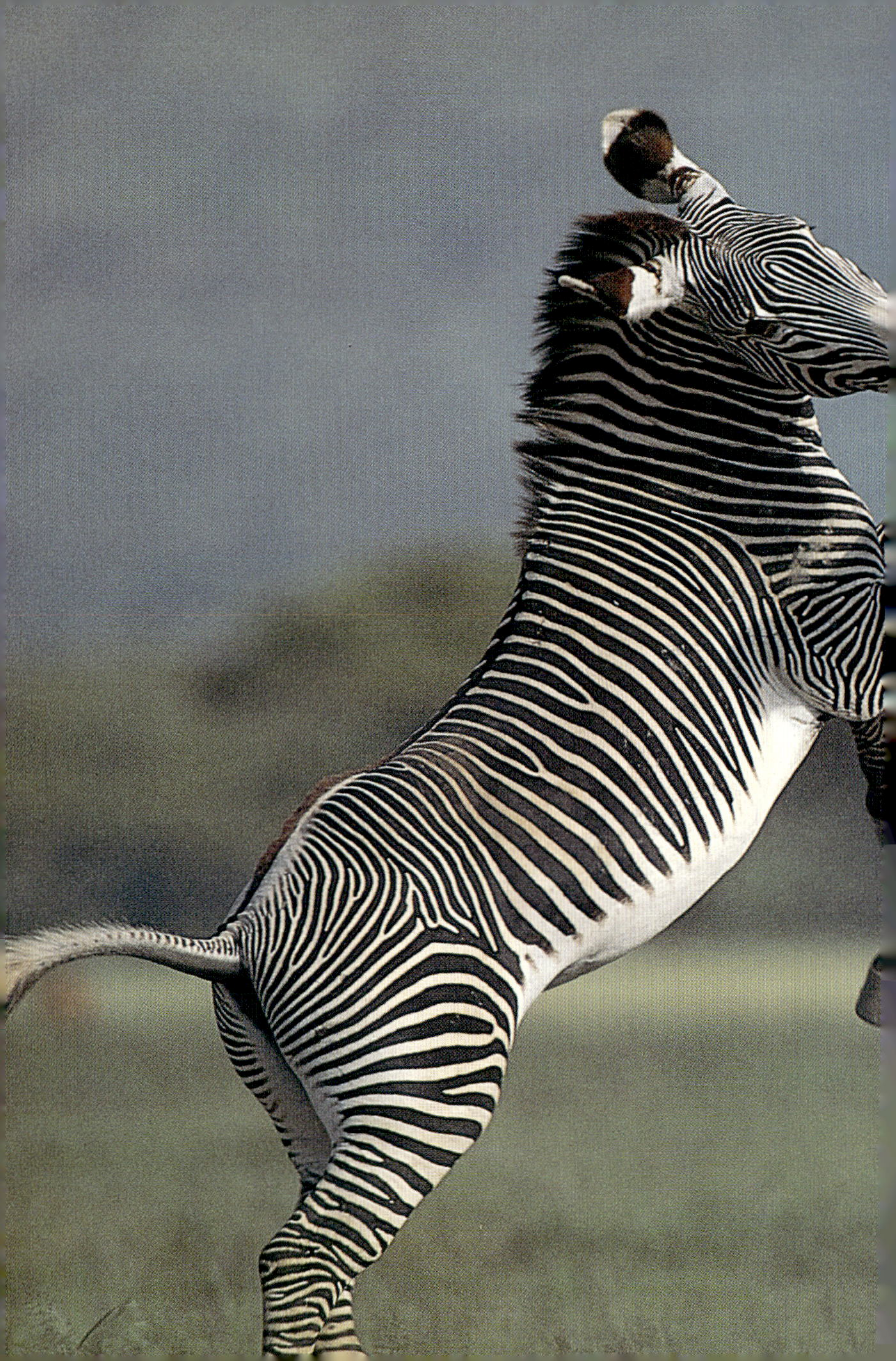

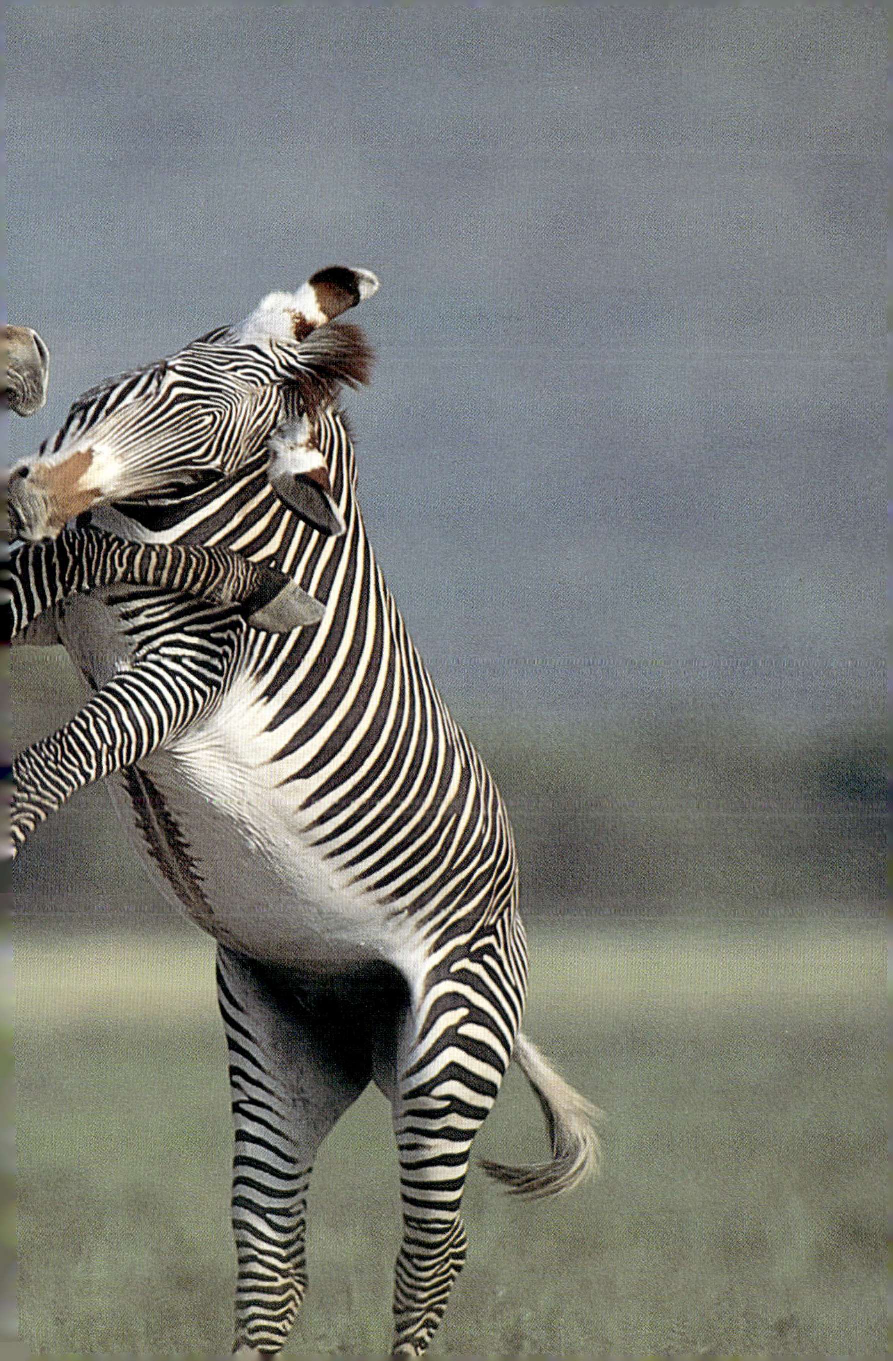

1. Gold, Frankincense and Myrrh

The Samburu, Shaba and Buffalo Springs National Reserves lie in Kenya's golden semi-desert north and together command a total area of 532 square kilometres. This is not yellow-sand desert, ridged by shifting dunes as in Arabia, Namibia or the Sahara, but dry, sparsely grassed flatlands, punctuated by dramatic hills and rugged mountains. Across vast areas the landscape is freckled with thornbush and scattered with stones and clusters of ancient rocks. Except after rare rains, when they burst into an exuberance of emerald green, leafless acacia trees somehow survive long periods of unremitting drought and are weighed down by the nests of colonies of weaver-birds. With every breath of the scorching inland wind the nests sway precariously, choreographed by nature into an entrancing aerial ballet.

On the approach to the three reserves, donkeys graze the meagre, dust-laden greenery and great numbers of voracious goats and fat-tailed sheep scrounge keenly for anything edible. In these mixed collections, often referred to facetiously as 'shoats', the colours of the goats set them apart: white, cream, beige, tan, chestnut, sable, black and piebald and dappled mixtures. Tails are another distinguishing factor. Those of the sheep hang down and, if very fat, hinder service. The goats' tails are always up, exposing all in the females and encouraging it.

Competing in the search for food, camels, some tethered in scant shade but many wandering freely, lend the scene an almost biblical ambience, especially when seen being driven in single file across the lonely distances towards the few existing waterholes — the rights to which are fiercely guarded. The scriptural evocation is reinforced by the bony, barefooted, and often long-robed herdsmen driving the camel trains, for these are the lands of gaunt, wiry people. The nomads of Kenya's north are accustomed to the hardships of their environment and it is rare to find a really fat man, woman or child among them.

The Uaso Nyiro — the Red (or Brown) River — is the lifesource of the three reserves and a boundary for each of them, dividing the Samburu from the Buffalo Springs reserve and forming the northern boundary of Shaba. Its name is found variously on old maps — even on more recent ones — as Gwaso Nyiro, Wuaso Ng'iro, Ewuaso Ng'iro, Ewaso Nyiro and Uaso Nyiro.

As hot, dry and desert-like as Kenya north of the equator may seem to many of its first-time visitors, the wild, lonely, often harsh beauty of it inevitably draws them back, a complete contrast with the modern way of life. The very air seems golden. In the days of the colonial administration, district and provincial officers became so attached to the untamed environment, its fiery climate and its people that they didn't know what to do with their lives when they retired. Having lived among them for years, their deeply-rooted loyalties and affections were with the Samburu, Boran, Sakuye, Turkana, Orma, Gabra, Rendille and part-Somali people, and it did not always make them popular with their masters.

Early mornings dawn copper-gold in the north — the name Shaba translates as copper — the huge sky subtly merging into yellow and platinum with the swift sunrise of the equator. Silhouetted against the sky's brightening expanse, bizarre-shaped hills and craggy mountains loom mysteriously, etched first in charcoal, changing, as the light catches them, to the burnt-gold, bronze, ochres and silver greys of their natural stone. The leaves of the palms and acacias along the river bank are tinged with gold and, behind them, the shapes of the hills and mountains are like those drawn by small

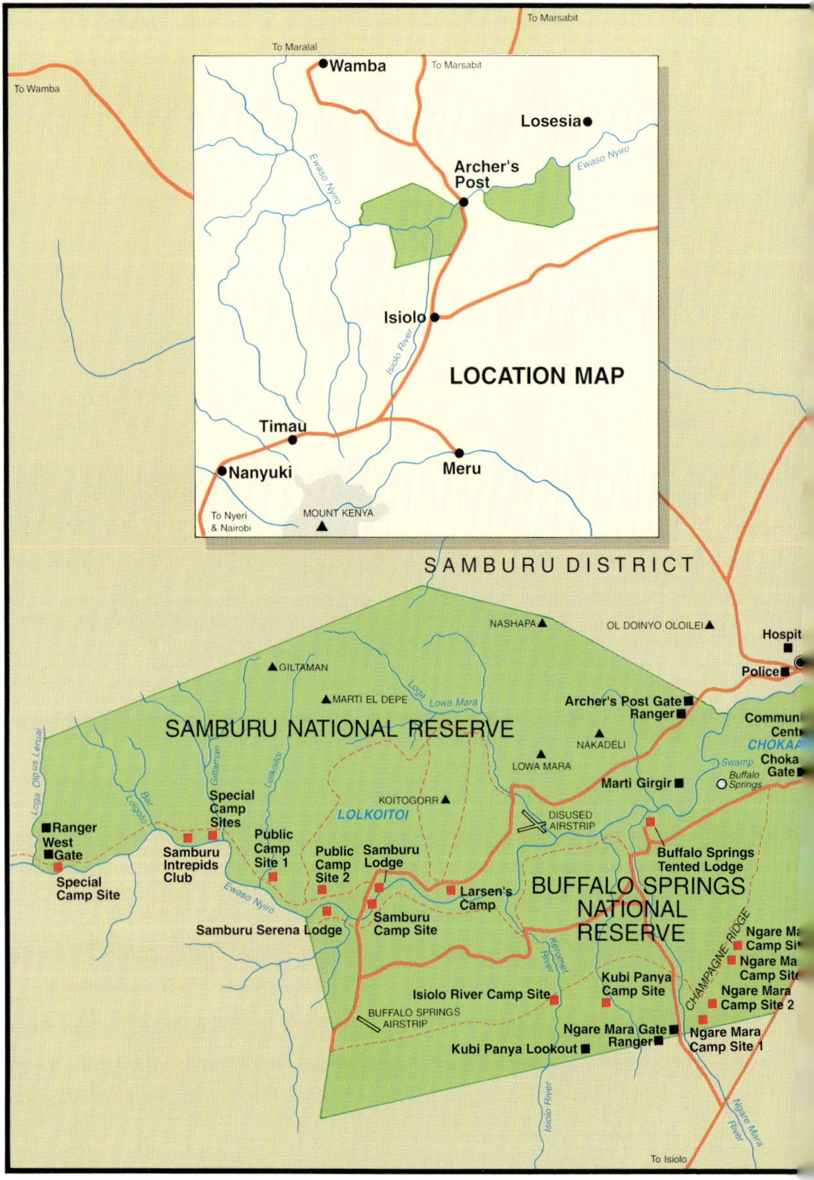

To Marsabit
To Maralal
To Wamba
Wamba
To Marsabit
Losesia
Archer's Post
Ewaso Nyiro
Ewaso Nyiro
Isiolo
Isiolo River
LOCATION MAP
Timau
Nanyuki
Meru
MOUNT KENYA
To Nyeri & Nairobi
SAMBURU DISTRICT
NASHAPA
OL DOINYO OLOILEI
GILTAMAN
MARTI EL DEPE
Loga Lowa Mara
Archer's Post Gate
Ranger
Police
SAMBURU NATIONAL RESERVE
NAKADELI
LOWA MARA
Swamp
Buffalo Springs
Marti Girgir
KOITOGORR
LOLKOITOI
DISUSED AIRSTRIP
Loga Olpus Lenuai
Bar Loigoto
Giltaman
Lolkoitoi
Ranger
West Gate
Special Camp Site
Samburu Intrepids Club
Special Camp Sites
Public Camp Site 1
Public Camp Site 2
Samburu Lodge
Ewaso Nyiro
Larsen's Camp
Buffalo Springs Tented Lodge
BUFFALO SPRINGS NATIONAL RESERVE
Samburu Serena Lodge
Samburu Camp Site
Keromet River
CHAMPAGNE RIDGE
Isiolo River Camp Site
Kubi Panya Camp Site
Ngare Mara Camp Site 2
BUFFALO SPRINGS AIRSTRIP
Ngare Mara Gate
Ranger
Ngare Mara Camp Site 1
Kubi Panya Lookout
Isiolo River
Ngare Mara River
To Isiolo

Samburu, Buffalo Springs & Shaba National Reserves

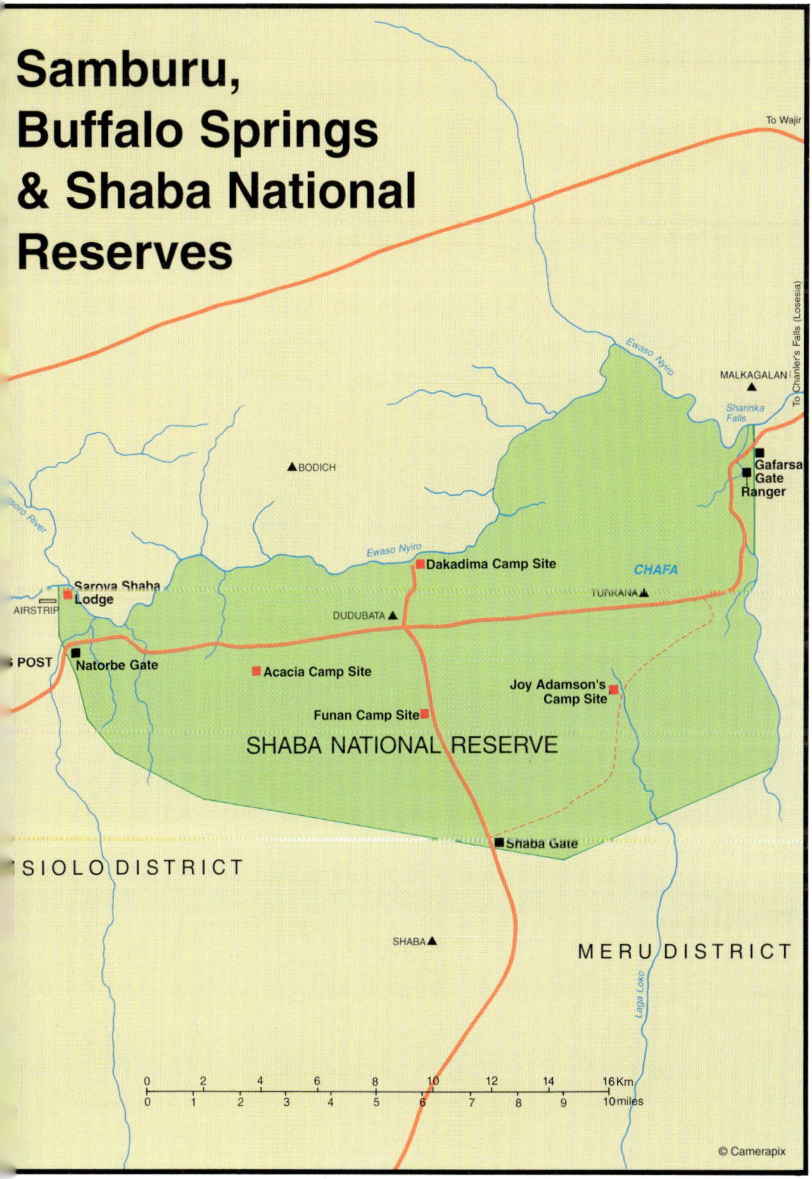

children — rounded, flat-topped and pyramid — some a solitary and awesome massif, others, like the Nyambenis, rolling along in a series of humps as if undecided for all eternity about where to start and where to stop.

Many are so ridged and eroded by the weathering of centuries that their curiously patterned walls seem to have been sculpted by some mighty hand. Others are half-clad in the green of sparse bush, or remain unadorned ancient naked rock — relics of another age.

The lands out of which they rise vary from startling white through silver or pale gold sand to stretches of apricot-coloured earth — vistas to tempt water-colourists. The shades, more apparent at sun-up and sundown, are almost bleached out of existence in the overall blinding whiteness of the middle of the day.

Even the stones here are memorable, again of many shapes, sizes and colours, by the roadside and in the dried-up river beds. These are the lands where a small stone pile miles from anywhere may indicate a lonely burial ground. Instead of leaving the dead and dying to be devoured by the hyenas, as is generally more customary — particularly with the nomadic Samburu people — a body was once laid here, either on the ground or in a shallow grave, and a few loose stones and rocks were heaped casually on top. For all the years into the future, passers-by who remembered the place and the person (and many others who did not) would cast another contribution, until the small cairn became a landmark, beneath which some long-dead nomad sleeps an everlasting sleep, at one with the stones and earth. Everywhere there is the sweet smell of the sun-baked grasses and herbs for throughout the three reserves the trees and bushes of the Burseraceae family flourish: *Boswellia neglecta* (used during Samburu circumcision rites) and *Boswellia carteri*, from the resin of

Overleaf: Cheetah are often seen on the Buffalo Springs side of the Uaso Nyiro River.

which frankincense is extracted, and the *Commiphora abyssinica* and *Commiphora africana*, from both of which myrrh is obtained.

Ivory, frankincense and myrrh from this eastern side of Africa were traded with the outside world before the birth of Christ and, as simple, natural air-fresheners, fragrant woods and grasses have been burned since time beyond memory in the humblest of homes, permanent or semi-permanent, from Isiolo to the Somali border and beyond.

Commiphora africana (Mbambara in Kiswahili), the thorny, velvet-leafed Samburuland shrub or small tree with pinkish-red fruit, is indigenous throughout northern Kenya, its green flowers growing in tight clusters and turning to red. Between five to ten metres in height it thrives in these parts because the herbivores avoid it, disliking its bitter tannin taste and yet, strangely, *Commiphora* wood is widely used for making cattle drinking troughs.

A decoction from the brown, almost black, bark of the *Acacia eliator* trees, which grow up to forty metres high along the Uaso Nyiro, is used to treat diarrhoea.

The *Acacia tortillis*, twenty metres high and almost always evergreen, produces pods and leaves attractive to both wild and domestic animals. The seketet bush (*Myrsine africana*) has medicinal qualities used for healing wounds and treating malaria.

The herbivores like the salt bush (*Salsola dandroides*). All the condiments, in fact, are available to the animals of Samburuland who take their pick of pepper-flavoured grasses, salt from the *Salsola* and mustard from the 'Toothbrush Tree', the *Salvadora persica* — Msuaki in Kiswahili — from which twigs shredded at the ends make natural toothbrushes.

Doum palms, the *Hyphaene compressa* — Mkoma in Kiswahili —

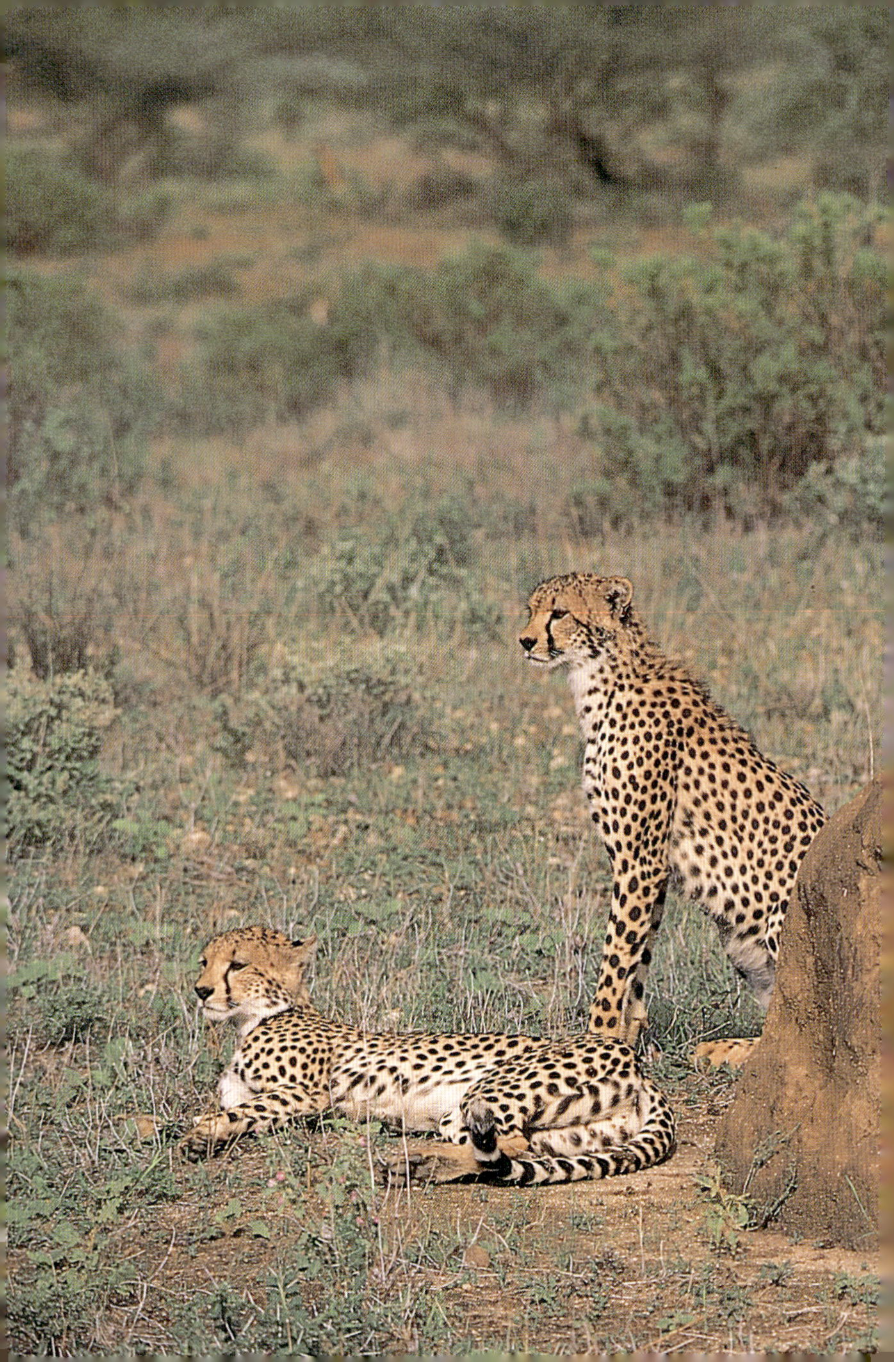

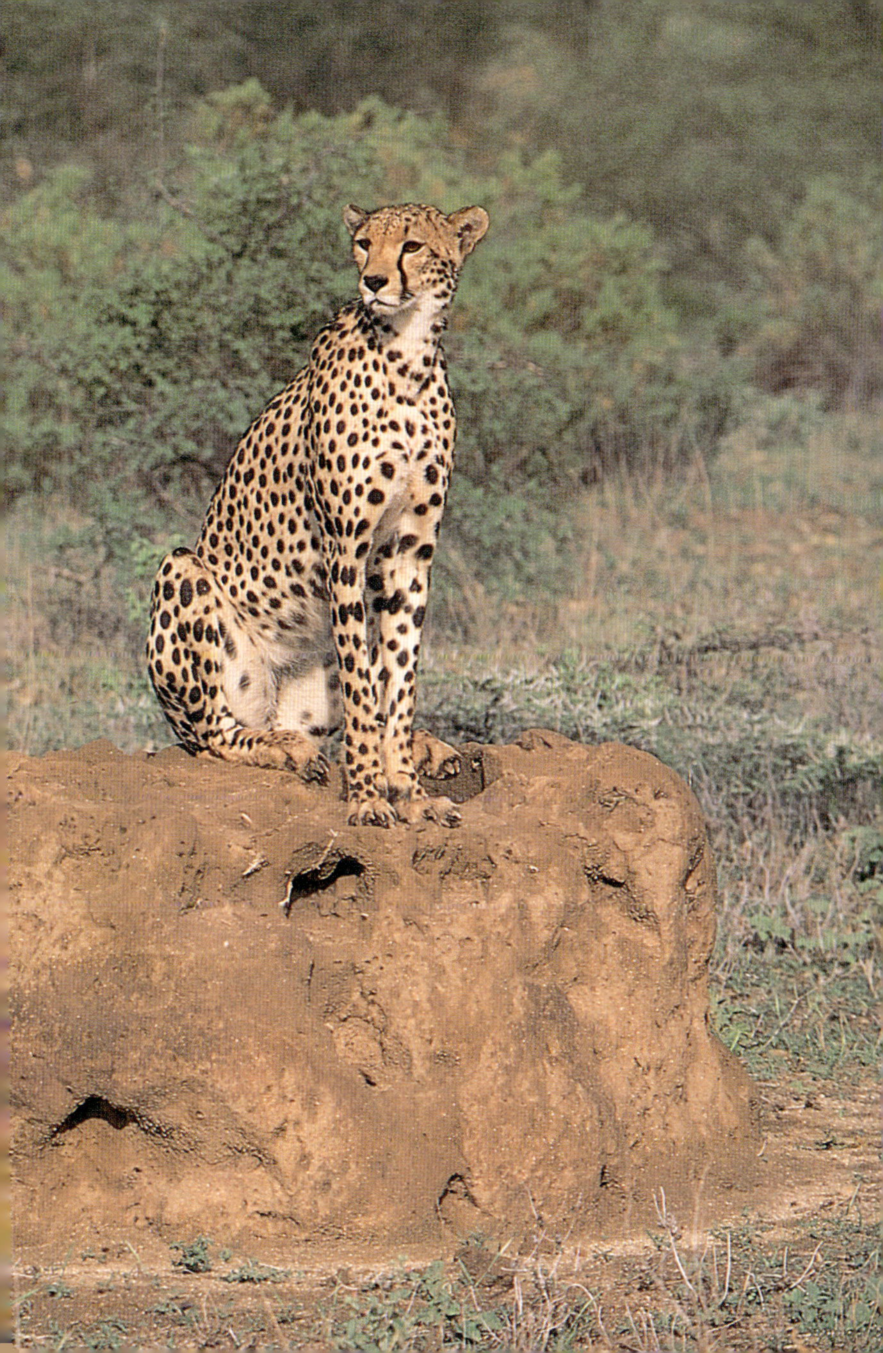

green the countryside wherever there is water, visible or underground. Elephants are partial to their great orange-coloured clusters of fruit, eating them whole and widely distributing the seeds in great mounds of dung. Each elephant dropping is the size and shape of a football and it is known that one enterprising local man's ambition is to encapsulate these massive heaps in clear plastic to sell to tourists as unusual mementos from Kenya . . . doum palm seeds and all.

Fibre from the doum palm leaves has been adopted recently in place of giraffe tail hair to make the *mporro* necklaces of Samburu married women.

Any available foliage is used to make nomad huts wherever they are wanted, the brushwood framework plastered over with mud and cow dung. Whatever of this humble home is portable, is loaded onto the backs of their donkeys when the time comes to move on.

Fibres from the pounded leaves of the *Sansevieria,* the wild sisal, are used to make mats for domestic use and sale.

Brilliant colour is brought to the drylands by one of nature's miracles, the beautiful desert rose, the *Adenium obesum,* which explodes onto the parched landscape of all three reserves in shades of pink through to deepest rose — whether or not rain has fallen.

In November and December the *Erythrinas* — the cork bark or 'lucky bean' trees burst into flower with glowing scarlet pannicles. The 'lucky beans' are their tiny, shiny, bright-red seeds smartly capped with glossy black, attractive in necklaces but extremely hard to pierce. They make pretty souvenirs although they are said to contain minute amounts of poison. Not seen for many years for sale in the bazaars and curios shops have been these seeds, cored and de-capped, enclosing a minuscule elephant, carved from ivory or bone.

Overleaf: With what appears to be little effort, the dances of Samburu moran *include exuberant straight-legged leaps from the ground.*

To keep the pygmy pachyderm captive, the cap is then carefully fixed back on.

The river, trees, herbs, grasses and — less pleasantly, but by nature's laws each other — sustain the wildlife of these golden lands.

Beyond the reserved areas, the most vibrant colours of Samburuland, often romantically called Kenya's 'Gateway to the North', are provided by the human element, the Samburu people themselves, believed by many to be the most handsome in the land.

Semi-nomadic pastoralists, ever in search of grazing for their large flocks and herds, groups often cluster around the trading centres and along the access routes to the three parks. Spectacular to the western eye — the tribe numbers just under 134,000 — only a small proportion lives in these semi-desert parts. The majority prefer the higher country offering better grazing for their stock: the Lorogi Plateau, the Mathews Range, the Ndotos and the slopes of Mount Nyiru further north.

Nilotes, like their cousins the Maasai and, like them also Maa-speaking, the Samburu people were originally neither indigenous to Kenya nor cattle-owning, but were driven southwards towards the Uaso Nyiro River out of the Sudan, Ethiopia or even further north. In the distant past they were hunters and the owners of large flocks of sheep and goats, calling themselves the *Il Oibor kineji*, 'the people of the white goats'. It was the Maasai who called them the *Isamburr* — the carriers of *samburrs* or traditional leather hunting bags — from which their name derives, although for many years it was thought that the name was inspired by the beautiful butterflies of Samburuland which, like the Samburu people, flit from place to place.

The Wandorobo hunters and gatherers scattered in small groups throughout Samburuland, more recently known by the name they

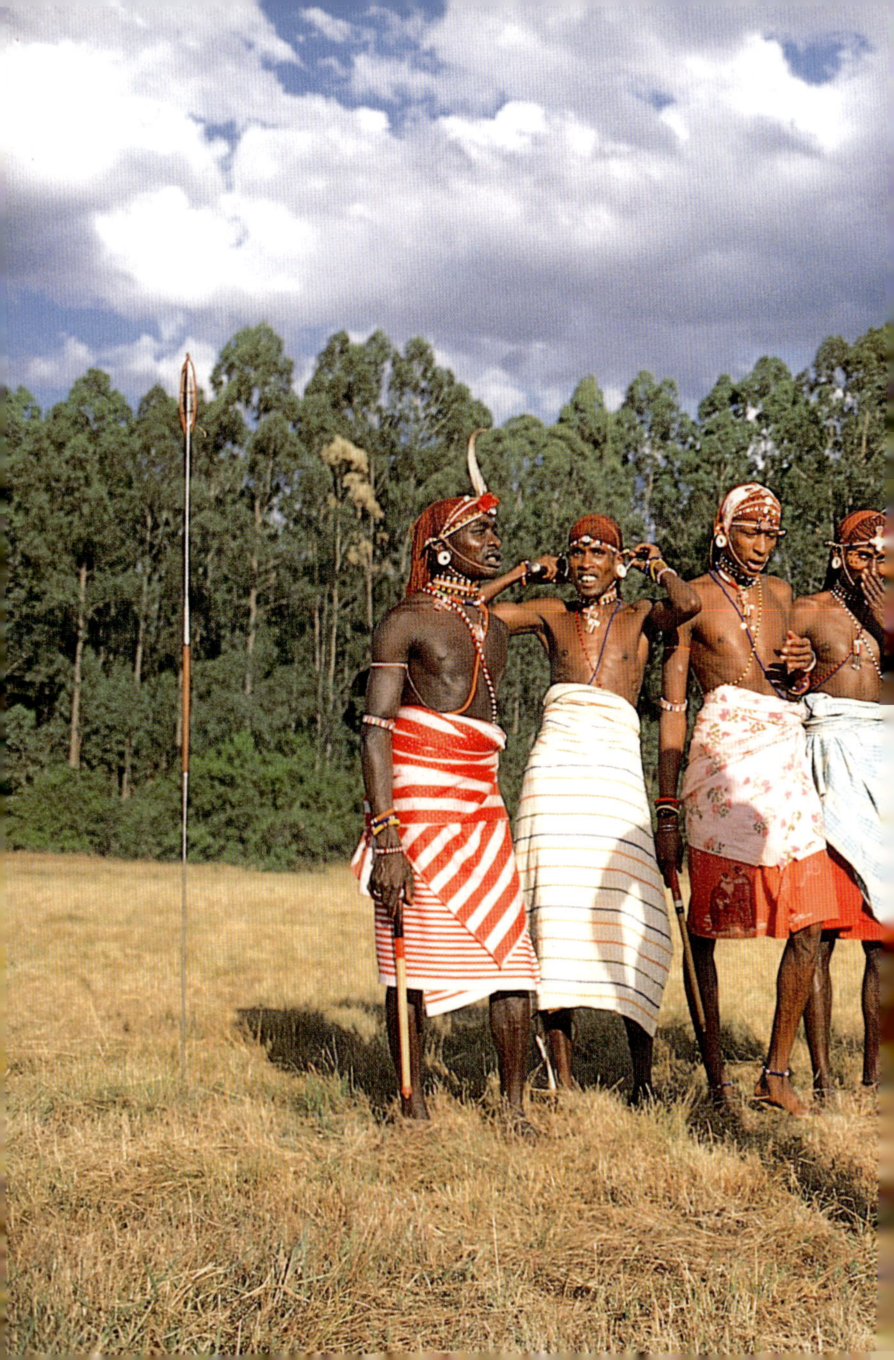

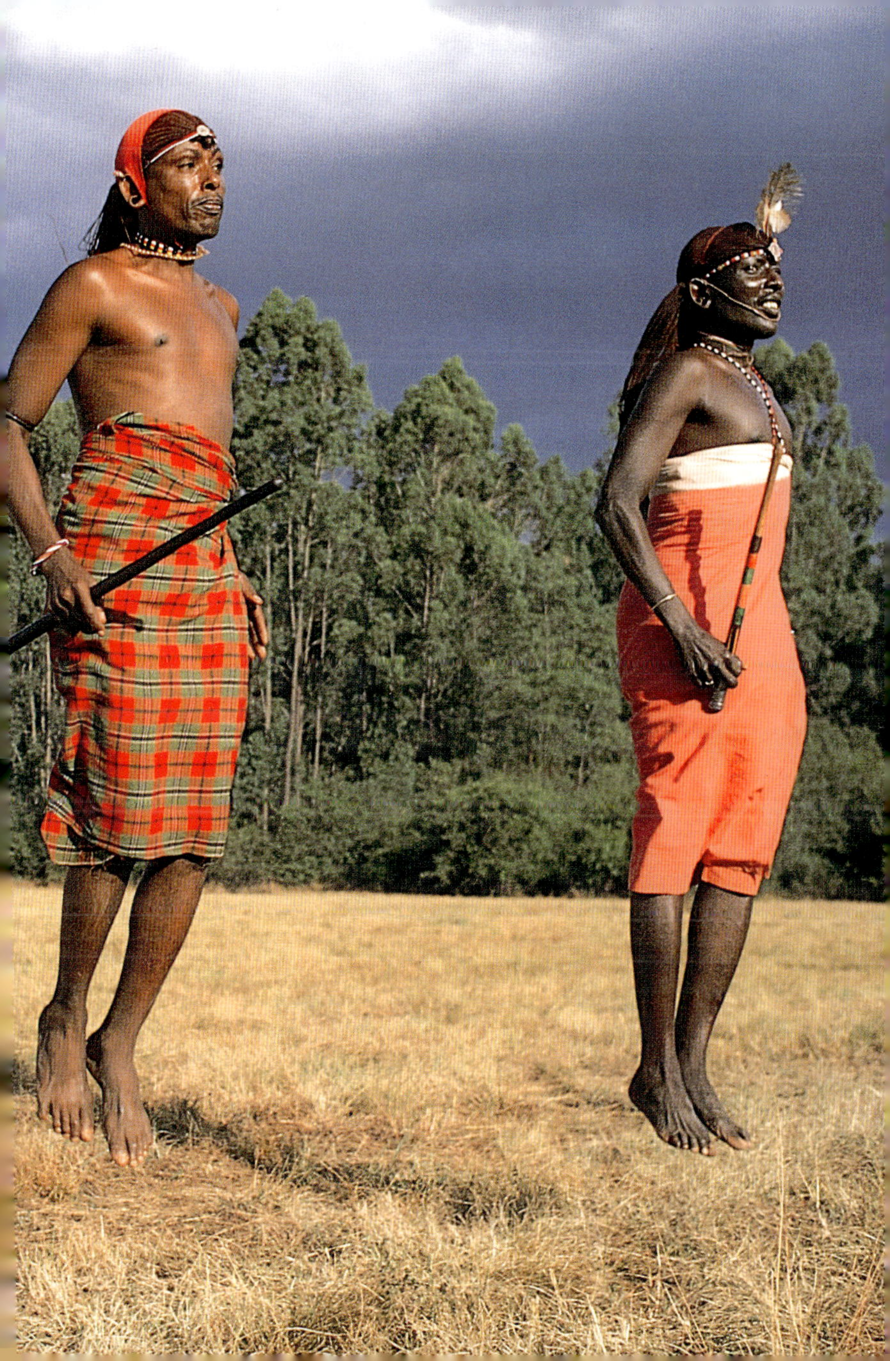

prefer — the Okiek — are also a Nilotic people. Living on wild fruits and edible plants and hunting with dogs outside the reserved areas, they are the honey-gatherers. Tiny in stature, compared with other Nilotic tribes, the Wandorobo still dress in skins and hunt with bows and arrows and can understand and 'talk' to the birds and the beasts.

The Nilotes were not the only tribes to reach and 'settle' — as much as nomadic people anywhere can 'settle' — in northern Kenya. The NFD — Northern Frontier District as it used to be called — covers almost half the country. The Cushitic people were also driven southwards: the cattle- and camel-owning Boran and the camel-owning Rendille, the Sakuye, Orma and Gabra.

A Rendille was regarded as 'poor' unless he owned a hundred camels or more and, when the 'Northern Frontier' was established along Kenya's borders with Ethiopia and Somaliland, it was to protect the nomadic desert tribes on the Kenya side — the Samburu, Turkana, Pokot, Rendille, Boran, Gabra and Somali immigrants — from armed Ethiopian ivory and cattle raiders. Even then, Samburu and Rendille pastoralists grazing their stock along the Uaso Nyiro were constantly raided by the Maasai, who believe that their God, *Enkai*, gave all cattle to them.

The Samburu had begun accumulating their own cattle herds, in addition to their sheep and goats, before crossing over into Kenya and, sometimes through intermarriage with the Cushitic tribes, gradually became the owners also of camels for their milk and as pack animals. A camel was a very acceptable bride-price, but many a poor beast died, in the beginning, because the Samburu had no knowledge of camel-care. Progress came when the camel purchase included a Rendille or Boran camel-minder, accustomed to the creature's peculiar ways.

The number of Rendille people in north-eastern Kenya is estimated at about 40,000. The Boran, probably more than 70,000, many of them Muslim converts, and the Sakuye, who number just over 3,000, herd their cattle, camels, sheep and goats south of the Uaso Nyiro down as far as Isiolo. The Orma, by 1992 believed to number more than 60,000, were originally driven down through Somalia, to inhabit the country to the east of Samburuland along the Tana River. More than 55,000 camel-herding Gabra, who also keep cattle, sheep and goats, occupy the lands to the north and east of Marsabit.

What the Samburu people lack in conventional clothing they make up for in the magnificently decorative traditional ornamentation of their women and the bright cloths — favouring tangerine and flame colours and hot reds — with which, sometimes toga-style, both the men and women drape themselves. Glamour for the young warriors comes with the cosmetic use on face and body of ochre mixed with fat. The men's elaborate coiffures, so precious to Samburu tradition, are believed to have been adopted from the Turkana tribes who, at the time of the Samburu people's long trek southwards, savagely plundered their herds as they grazed them north of Mount Kulal.

Several years ago, when invited to enter competitors in an international beauty contest, Tanzania's first president Julius Nyerere refused to let his country be represented, stating: 'ALL our people are beautiful, providing they are well fed.' True enough. Yet Kenya's Samburu people, with their fine, aristocratic features and splendid athletic physiques, surviving mainly on a frugal diet of milk and blood tapped from their domestic beasts, supplemented only occasionally by a meal of meat, are undisputedly among the most handsome and beautiful people of the African continent.

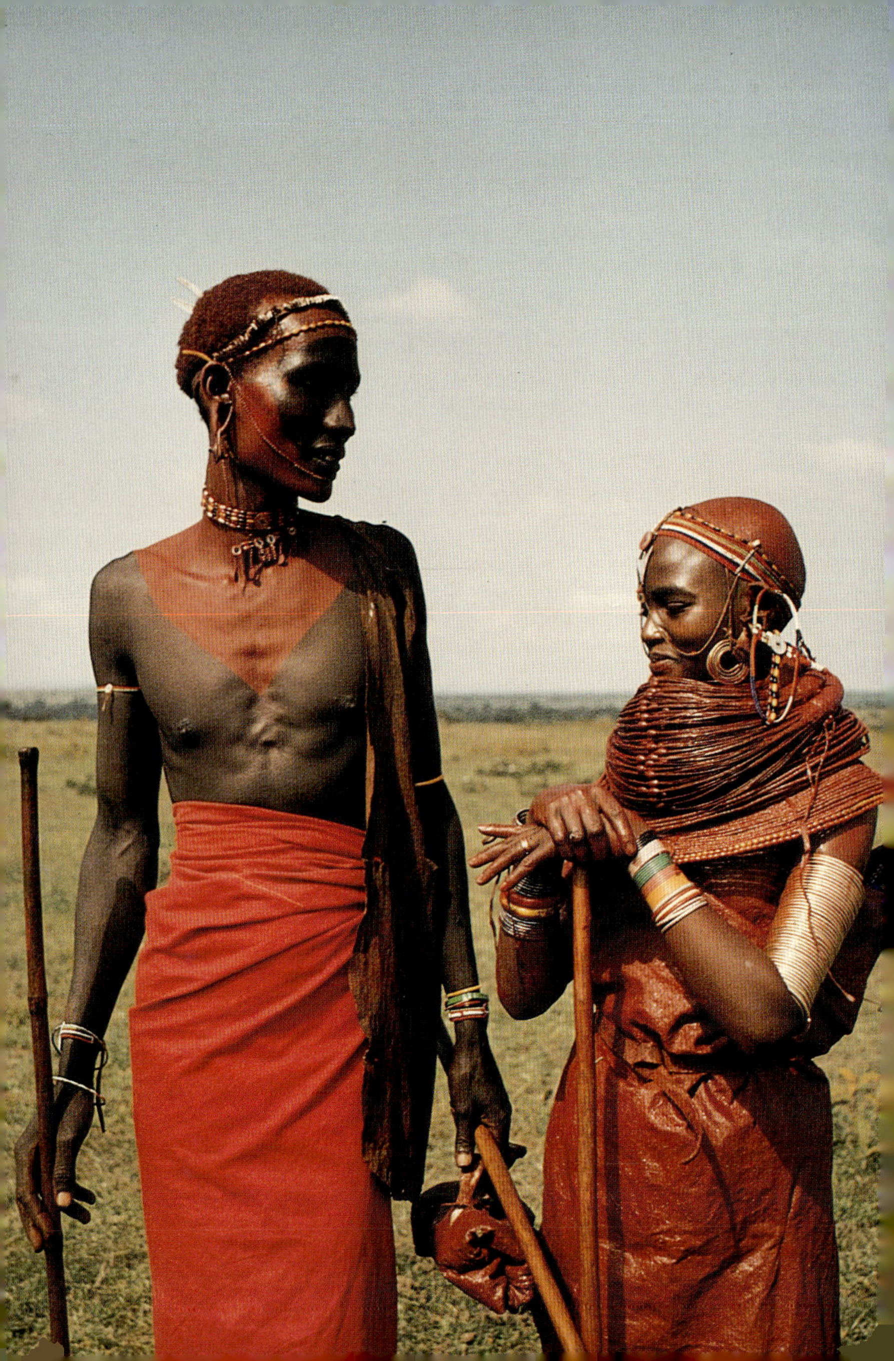

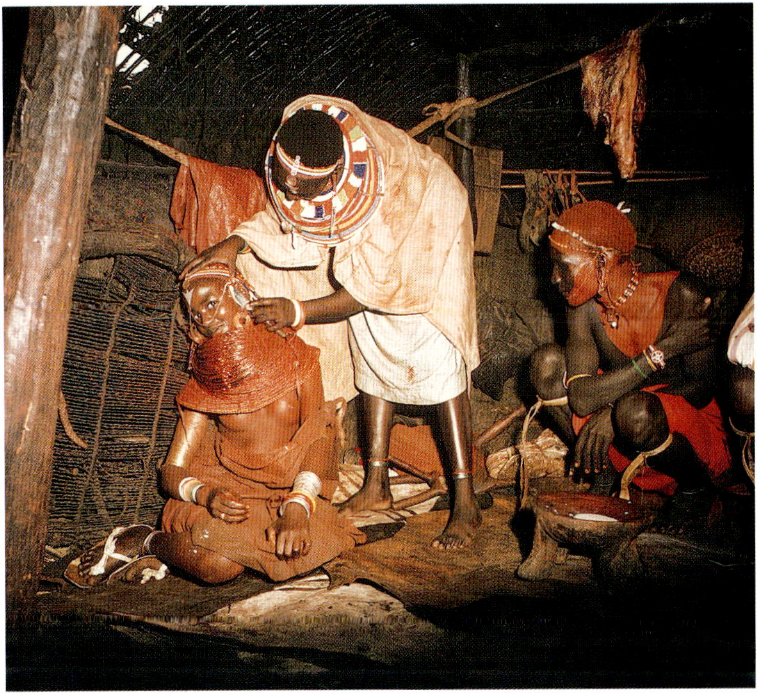

Above: In the bridal hut, much attention is given to making the bride-to-be look her best.

Right: Women prepare the day's meal in the manyatta.

Opposite: A Samburu couple on their wedding day. No longer a moran *the groom can no longer wear his hair stylishly long. The bride's head is shaved.*

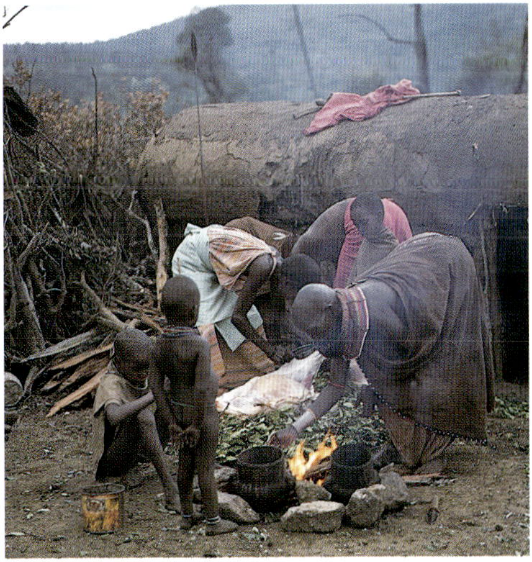

Withstanding the heat and the waterless wastes with the common aim of finding sufficient grazing and water for the herds and flocks which are the sole representatives of their individual and collective wealth, the Samburu and their neighbours have endowed the golden lands they inhabit north and south of the Uaso Nyiro River with a rich cultural and religious mix.

*Opposite: Gerenuk (*Litocranius walleri*) stand up on their hind legs to reach the newer shoots of whatever desert trees and shrubs they can find.*

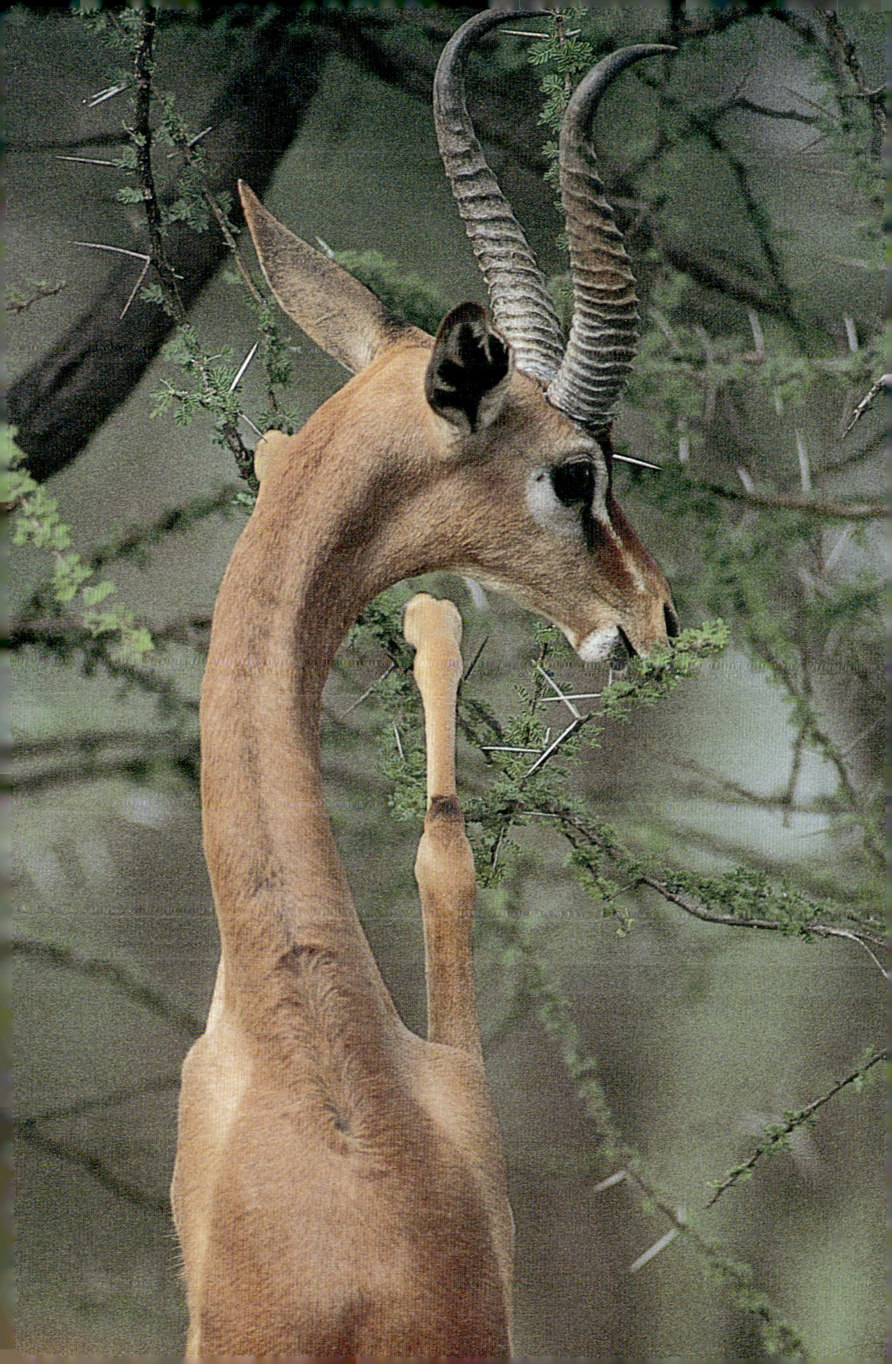

2. The Uaso Nyiro a century ago

Until the last decade of the nineteenth century, Kenya's north was virtually cut off from the rest of the world. For the earliest adventurers into the area, making their own maps as they went along, the mountains and the Uaso Nyiro River were the most identifiable landmarks to help them on their way and it was a part of what the Europeans called the great 'Dark Continent' that was just crying out for exploration.

Four expeditions took place after the Scottish explorer Joseph Thomson blazed a trail from the coast to Lake Victoria through 'dreaded Masai country'. His account of his adventures in his book *Through Masai Land* opened the eyes of readers everywhere on great areas of 'undiscovered' territory.

Part of his brief from the Royal Geographical Society was to report on Mount Kenya and its surroundings, and it was from his camp on a bend of the Uaso Nyiro that, almost missing it because of heavy cloud, he saw it 'as the sun set in the western heavens'.

Rising below Ol Doinyo Lesatima — at 3,999 metres the highest peak of the Aberdares range to Samburuland's south-west — the Uaso Nyiro is fed by countless tributaries along its north-easterly course and, from the northern fringes of the Buffalo Springs and Shaba National Reserves, by many bubbling springs. Believed to be from the melted snows of Mount Kenya, the waters filter down through lava and porous soil bringing green life to the drylands wherever they emerge. The spring water is clean and cool and crystal clear, only to lose itself in the wide, brown, winding river.

Doomed not to reach the sea, the Uaso Nyiro disappears into the Lorian Swamp south of Habaswein in the east, but all through this semi-desert country only fractionally north of the equator, sustains life for great distances beyond its banks for human beings, their

Overleaf: Doum palms make an imposing silhouette against the setting sun.

livestock, the indigenous wildlife, birds and reptiles. From the ground and from the air its course through the featureless bush is defined by a dark green snaking ribbon of riverine trees and plant life and some quite unexpected waterfalls. Two of these are the Sharinka Falls at the easternmost end of the Shaba reserve north of the Gafarsa Gate and, further east beyond the park, the picturesque cascade of Chanler's Falls.

Contrary to the general belief that Joseph Thomson named the magnificent upstream seventy-two-metre drop of Thomson's Falls for himself, he in fact named them for his father, whose only African experiences were through the eyes of his wandering boy. In Kenya, they are now more often called the Nyahururu Falls, a name meaning, in the Maa language of the Maasai, 'where the waters run deep'.

On their expedition to discover Lakes Rudolf (Turkana) and Stephanie (Chew Bahir) in 1887-88 — before which Lake Turkana's great watermass was known as 'Samburu' — the Hungarian nobleman Count Samuel Teleki von Szek, with the Austrian naval officer Ludwig von Höhnel, explored thirty-one miles of the Uaso Nyiro and camped on its banks. They found it to be 'broad and rapid though shallow', much as it is today. They also found it rich in fish. 'With three rods only,' von Höhnel recorded 'we landed some twenty big fellows in a very short time.' And those must have made a welcome change of diet for all.

Twenty-two-year-old William Astor Chanler's expedition was the next across these golden lands, approaching from the south-east. The son of the US Congressman John Winthrop Chanler, and great-great grandson of the American millionaire John Jacob Astor, he arrived in Zanzibar in March 1889 'bored with his studies at Harvard' and, 'merely for sport', spent six months in the Kilimanjaro region. It was

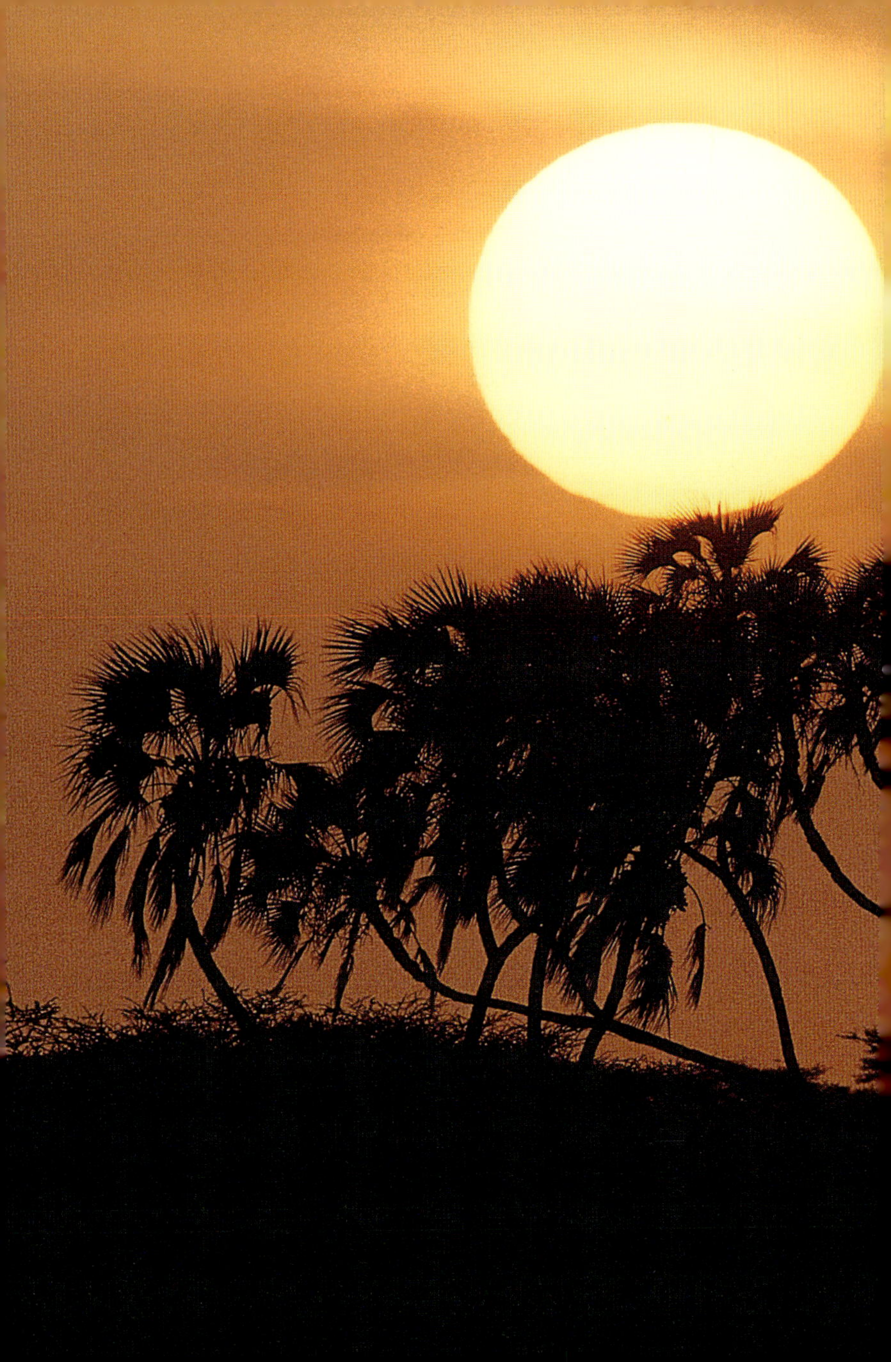

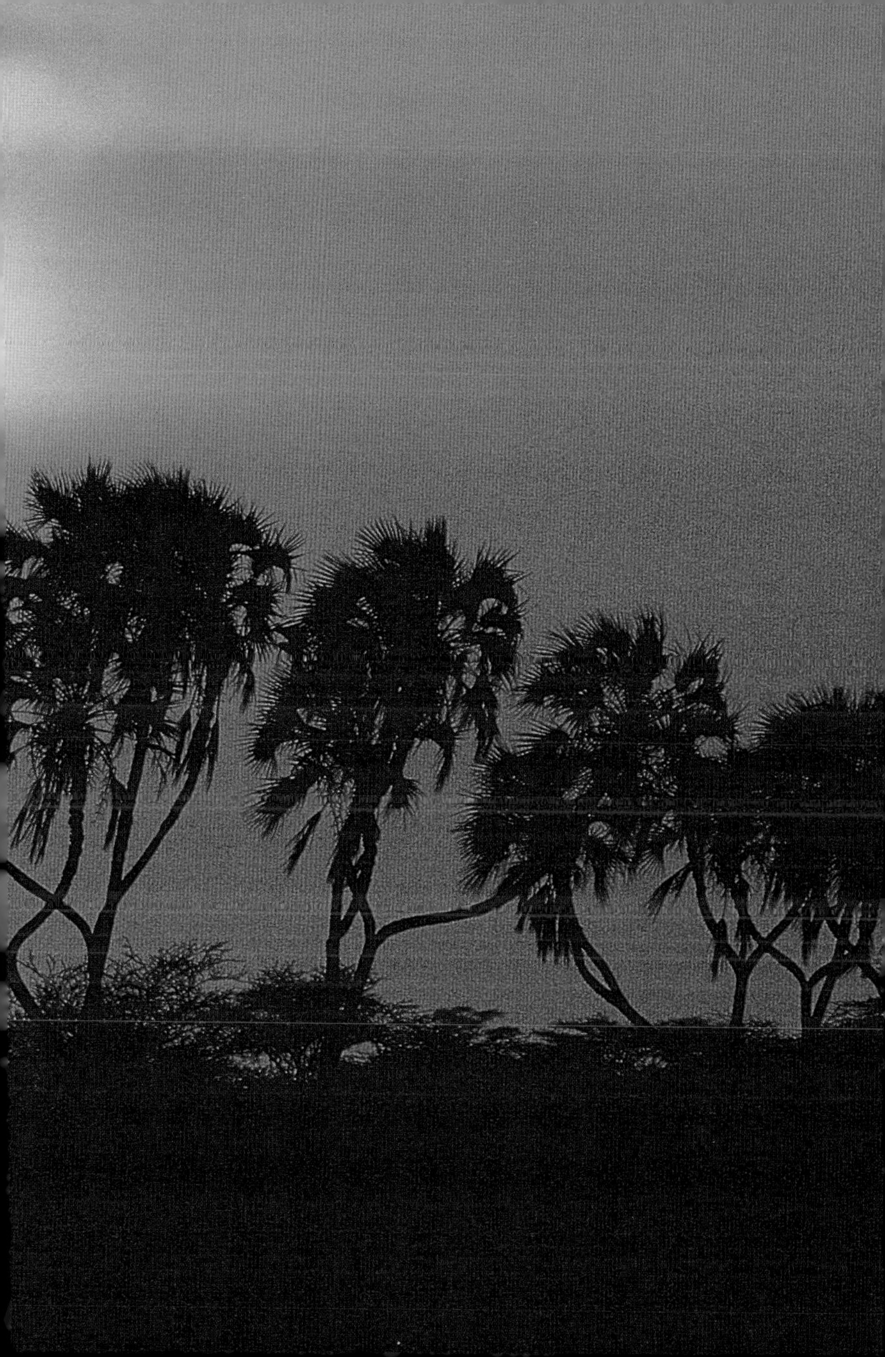

then that he decided to lead an expedition to Lake Rudolf and the Juba River.

By letter, and in a personal visit to Vienna, he was able to induce Ludwig von Höhnel to accompany him, though von Höhnel was still exhausted from his long, incapacitating walk with Teleki.

They left Europe separately for Aden where von Höhnel remained to recruit Somalis for the expedition while Chanler went on to Zanzibar to enlist porters. When von Höhnel saw the 135 men Chanler had assembled he felt grave misgivings, and not without good cause — as future events revealed.

But, led by Chanler, Chanler's eighteen-year-old servant and friend George Galvin, and von Höhnel, they left Lamu on Kenya's north-eastern seaboard on 18 September 1892 in a party of porters, Somali camel-drivers, Sudanese guards (armed with Mannlichers), donkeys, horses, three dogs, camels, oxen, goats and sheep — their peripatetic butcher's shop, as it were — to sustain their needs in the wilderness.

For two months they marched 402 kilometres inland beside the Tana River but had many desertions. When they reached the Nyambenis, south of Shaba, they hired a guide to take them to the 'Guaso Nyiro' and 'Lake Lorian', it always having been believed until then that the swamp was a large lake.

By now Chanler, extremely ill with malaria, was semi-conscious and delirious, but they reached the waterfall on the Uaso Nyiro on Boxing Day 1892 and, in naming it Chanler's Falls, immortalised the young American's name on all future maps and history books.

Their euphoria was short-lived. On 12 January they found that 'Lake Lorian', to their utter disappointment, was not a lake at all but a massive swamp of pools and reed beds extending over a vast area.

Overleaf: Nature in the raw. Lion pride on a Grevy zebra kill. The vultures will swoop down after them.

The river itself begins to disappear into it at Sericho, north-east of Chanler's Falls.

It was February 1893 before they staggered back to their base where, attacked by the waMeru, three of their porters were killed, twelve wounded, and they learned from Galvin, who had remained there to guard the camp, that many of their precious oxen, cattle, camels and donkeys had died.

The expedition continued north but, in August 1893, von Höhnel was badly gored by a rhino and had to be carried 400 kilometres south to the mission station at Kibwezi on the route back to the coast. From there, partially recovered, he returned to Vienna. Yet despite all its hardships he never really regretted his adventures in this wild and often hostile country. When he was subjected to crippling financial embarrassment in his latter years in Austria, William Astor Chanler never forgot him and helped to support him until the end of his days.

Local politics intervened when Chanler attempted to continue his trip to Lake Rudolf. 'The British didn't like the idea of an American marching around their unexplored territory carrying the American flag and decided to put a stop to it,' his nephew later reported.

Was the young American's expedition a failure? Hardly so in the records of exploration, for 965 kilometres of untrod territory had been covered. He had mapped the lower reaches of the Uaso Nyiro and had, once and for all, exploded the 'myth' of 'Lake Lorian'. He had also recorded for posterity the first sighting of Chanler's reedbuck (*Redunca fulvorufula chanleri*), similar to the Bohor reedbuck (*Redunca redunca wardi*) but greyer and with sandy legs and thighs. The first edition of his book *Through Desert and Jungle* was published in 1896.

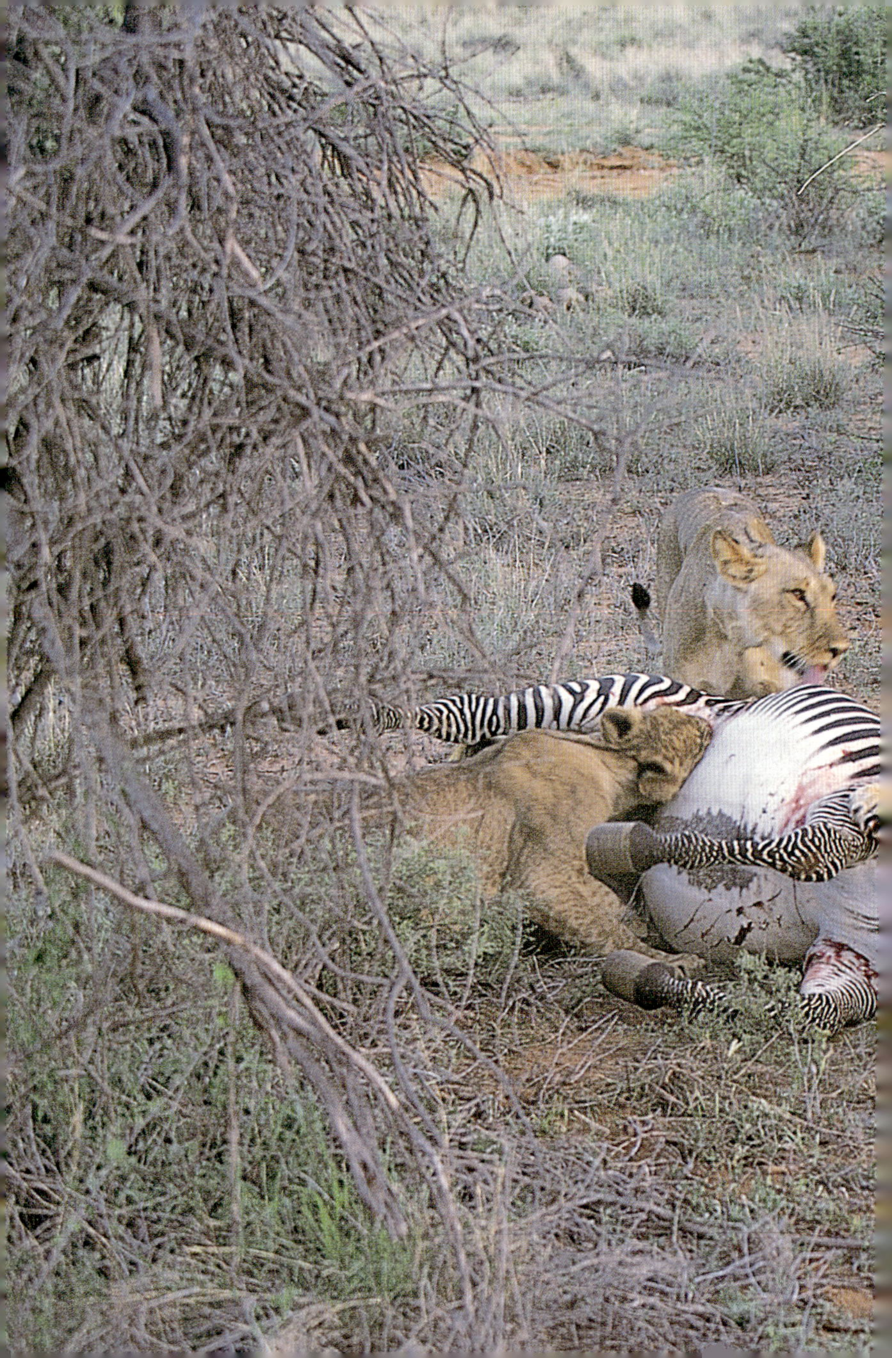

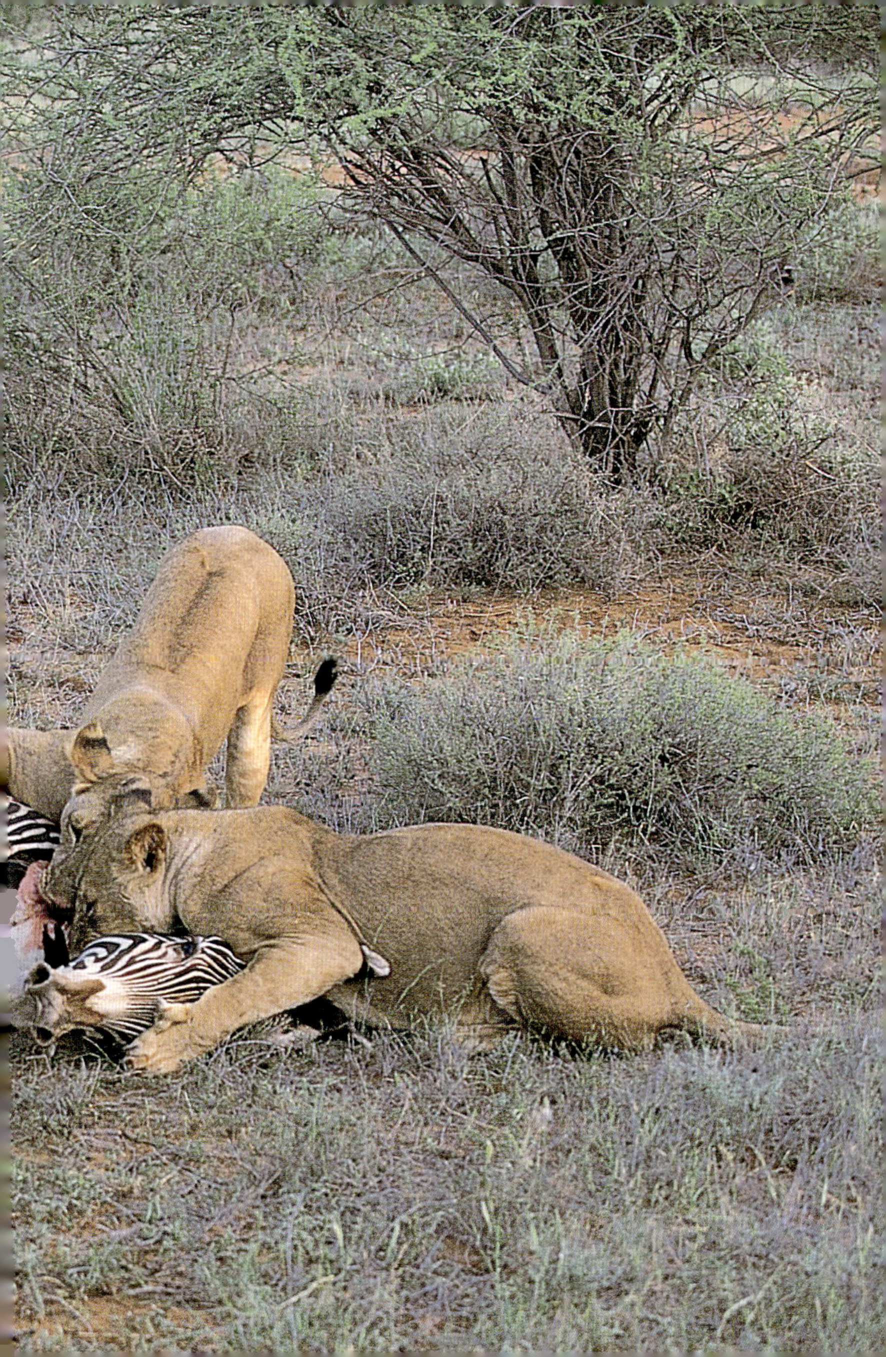

'He had much to be proud of,' Pascal James Imperato, MD, was to write in his detailed resumé: *Arthur Donaldson Smith and the exploration of Lake Rudolf*, published by the Medical Society of the State of New York in 1987. It sheds a new light on the early explorations of the country which was, after Chanler's and Donaldson Smith's time, to be known first as British East Africa and then as Kenya. Moreover, the Imperato publication contains route maps, safari pictures and portraits of the *dramatis personae* — Donaldson Smith, Chanler, Galvin and von Höhnel — revealing as much of their characters and personalities as the meticulously written text.

One tends to look back on the early explorers as the haggard, bearded, half-starved, ill and wild-eyed individuals often pictured returning from months, sometimes years, in 'the bush' but, in fact, Chanler, Galvin and Donaldson Smith (Donnie, always, to his family) were all good looking, very presentable young men; two of them wealthy in their own right.

Now the American Arthur Donaldson Smith, MD, comes onto the scene, to add his own contribution, as he himself put it, to 'the sea of knowledge'. Born into a well-to-do Pennsylvania family, he chose to drop the name of Arthur at an early age, preferring to be known simply as A. Donaldson Smith or, preferably, just Donaldson Smith — without the hyphen which so often erroneously appears in print.

He had been interested in natural history from early in life and it influenced his future while still young. At an incredibly early age he gained his medical degree in Pennsylvania in May 1889, did a year's postgraduate study at Heidelburg, but forsook his profession 'to pursue his love of adventure' after inheriting two-and-a-half million dollars on his father's death in 1892.

Before his father died he had been on hunting trips to Mexico and, with a friend also called Smith (no relation), to Norway. After the death of his father they both set off to hunt in Somaliland, following which Donaldson Smith made Lake Rudolf his next target, hoping to be the first white man to reach there after Teleki. Von Höhnel had only explored twenty-four kilometres north of the lake in 1888 and Donaldson Smith was keen to establish the lake's source.

Sailing from London to Berbera at the beginning of June 1894, he recruited fifty-five Somalis and, by marching nine hours each day, first covered the thirty-eight kilometres to Hargeisha then, following a route eastwards across the Webe Shebeli, Webe Ganana and Webe Daua rivers via Lake Abaya to Lake Stephanie (which he walked around), turned south down the eastern shores of Lake Rudolf to Marsabit, crossed the Uaso Nyiro and went south-east to Lamu on the coast.

In the event, it was the Italian explorer Captain Victor Bottego who finally proved that the source of Lake Turkana is the Omo River, not the Nianamm as had previously been thought.

Throughout his travels Donaldson Smith made detailed and extensive records of the wildlife encountered, affording us, for purposes of comparison, an interesting backward look on our 'golden lands' as they were then . . . hardly a tourist's paradise from Donaldson Smith's point of view.

He was struck by lightning; knocked unconscious while hunting Thomson's gazelle; fought with the Boran who were after his camels and mules; and was almost killed by an elephant. When he reached the Uaso Nyiro on 2 September 1895 he had 'traversed 140 miles of some of the most difficult terrain in Kenya'.

Recovering from malaria, he camped eight days at Melka Koja (a spot on the river banks which Chanler and von Höhnel had already

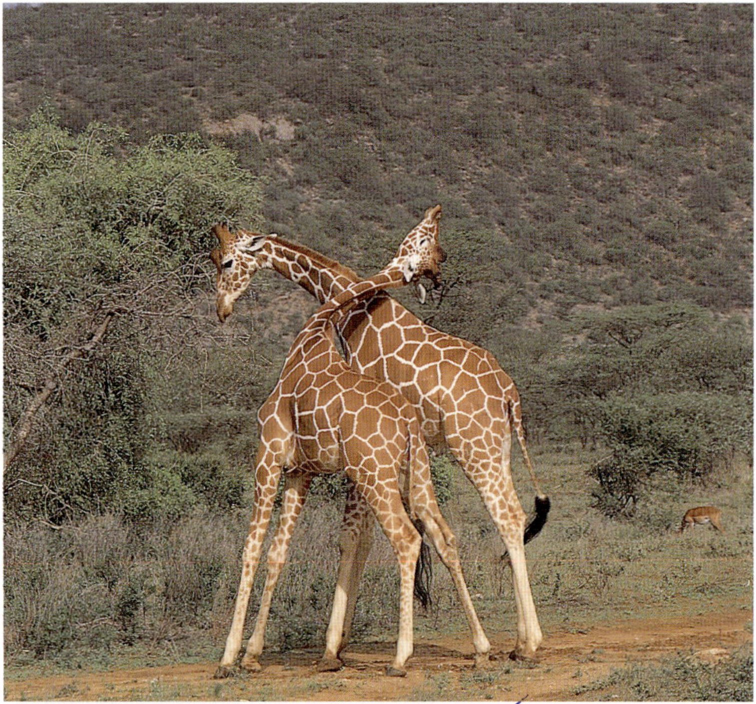

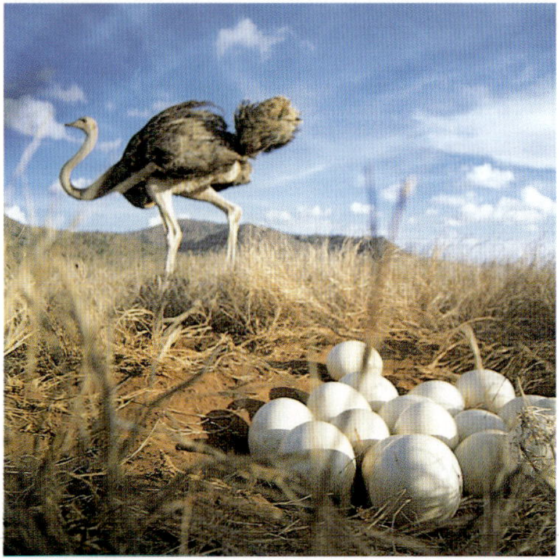

Above: Male Reticulated giraffe 'necking' or sparring, a form of fighting which goes on year-round.

*Left: The Somali ostrich of the north (*Struthio camelus molybdophanes*) has blue-grey neck and thighs. Like its cousin the Maasai ostrich, its clutches of eggs are laid directly on the ground.*

Opposite: Black rhino — as underestimated to his cost by the unfortunate Dr George Kolb.

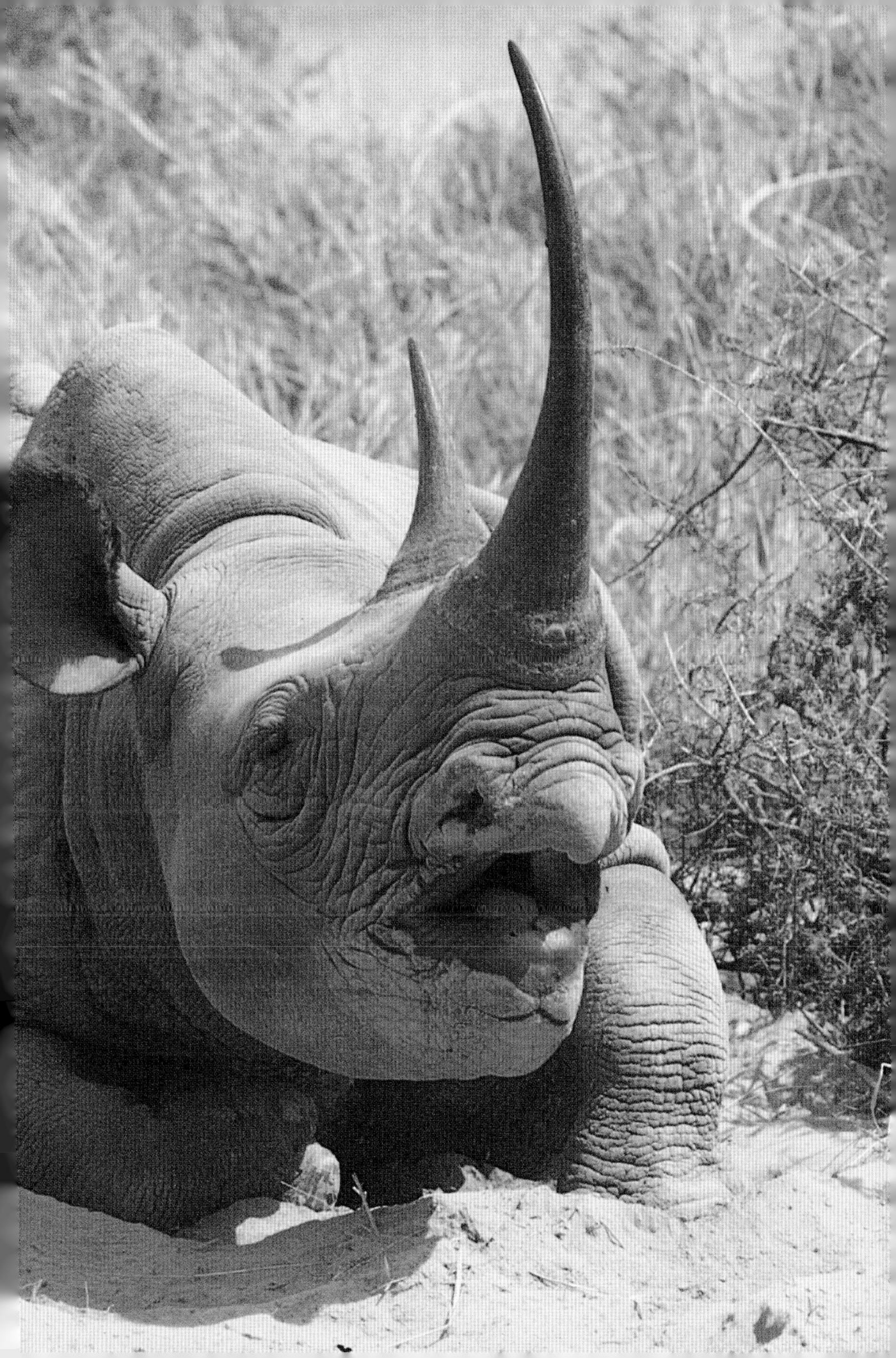

reached on their way to the Lorian Swamp) and, under the worst conditions, performed remarkable surgery on the arm of his most trusted Somali gunbearer Yusif, who was almost dragged away by a crocodile while carrying a sheep across the river. Donaldson Smith had no alternative but to amputate.

His records reveal that the country between the Uaso Nyiro and the Tana was full of rhino then. His total collection from the expedition was 700 specimens of birds, twenty-four of which were new to science; 300 reptiles and batrachians, of which eleven were new; 300 plant specimens; 1,000 butterflies; 200 mammals and close to 6,000 insects. On returning to England at the end of November 1895 he presented his findings to the Royal Geographical Society, donated all new species to the British Museum and the balance to the Academy of Natural Sciences of Philadelphia.

When he was in the far north, on the Kenya-Abyssinian (now Ethiopian) border, Karsha, a member of his camp staff, brought him a rare, crested tree rat which Donaldson Smith initially identified as 'resembling *Lophiomys imhausi*' but with which he himself was later credited — *Lophiomys smithii*. He was also credited with a bird (*Turacus donaldsoni*) and a fish (*Synodontis smithii*).

He gave to posterity his *Through Unknown African Countries*, a volume now long out of print, a collectors' item for many years and not easy to come by.

By much the same route, Donaldson Smith was followed to the Uaso Nyiro in 1896-97 by Lord Delamere (Hugh, the third baron), Kenya's pioneer settler who was convinced that this land of his choice was 'White Man's Country'. He almost succeeded in making it one but Delamere's journey was more in the nature of a hunting safari than an expedition.

Throughout his life accident prone, he was accompanied — at his mother's insistance — by Dr A E Atkinson. Both men were hunting mad and later settled in Kenya (British East Africa as it still was then). Delamere as both politician and farmer became a legend, but Atkinson was to opt for a less flamboyant career as a high-grade cattle breeder.

Approaching Kenya from the north-east, Delamere's route took him through the waterless Galla, Gabra, Boran, Rendille and Turkana country to Lake Turkana (Rudolf) and down the eastern side of the Turkwell River to Lake Baringo and Eldama Ravine. From there he reconnoitred a considerable length of the 'Ewaso Erok' and 'Ewaso Nyiro' rivers before cutting north again to Marsabit.

It was on the Uaso Nyiro that an ugly little drama took place. To Delamere's and Atkinson's surprise, for they were in deserted country, they overtook a small caravan of two German naturalists on their way to Meru to buy food. The two parties joined up, with Dr George Kolb, his companion, gunbearer and cook taking the forward position slightly ahead of the rest. Those behind heard the shout of *'Faru! Faru!'* (Rhino! Rhino!) from Kolb's gunbearer and, hurrying forward, found that both Dr George Kolb and his cook had been gored — Kolb fatally — by the enraged mother of a young rhino which Kolb had shot and wounded. Ironically, for Kolb was inordinately fond of rhinoceros liver and had killed scores of them for food, the rhino had thrust her horn right through the middle of his body and not even Atkinson's skill could save him. According to *Petermanns Mitteilungen* (1896) the naturalist had been the first to map much of what is now eastern Kenya.

The ground was too hard to receive Kolb's body so they covered him with the 'traditional' cairn of stones which was to be his only

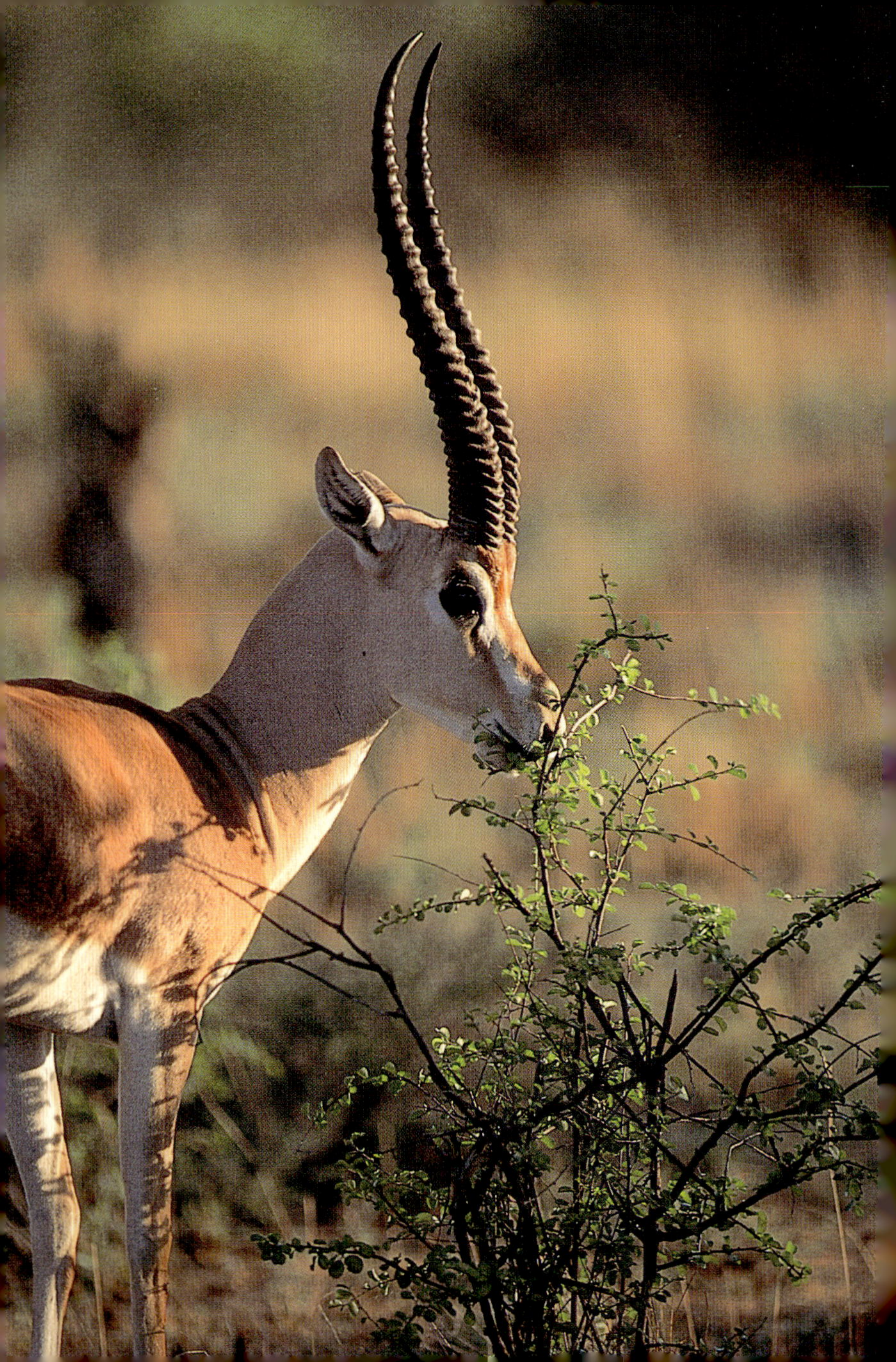

memorial in this faraway foreign land.

Tearfully, Kolb's companion wrote to his mother that night: 'We have buried our dear Doctor beneath a spreading mimosa [acacia] tree and the German flag flies over his grave.' The 'German flag' was, says Elspeth Huxley in *White Man's Country*, only a rather grubby piece of rag tied to a stick propped up by stones.

The 330-kilometre northern Uaso Nyiro — 'a river of the equatorial desert' as Theodore Roosevelt described it in 1909 — is a different river entirely from another Kenya river of the same name. The 140-kilometre southern Uaso Nyiro rises on the far side of the Great Rift Valley in the forested slopes of the Mau Escarpment and feeds the southern plains. Curiously, it too disappears into a swamp and never reaches the sea. This is the southern Ewaso Nyiro Swamp, which empties into Lake Natron in Tanzania.

Opposite: Male Grant's gazelle (Gazella granti) *similar to the Thomson's* (Gazella thomsoni) *but larger. Grant's seem impervious to the heat of a Samburu day and can survive without water for quite long periods if they have to.*

Overleaf: Tussle in the bush. Elephants (Loxodonta africana) *have always favoured Samburu because of the Uaso Nyiro River. They need to drink not less than 136 litres a day.*

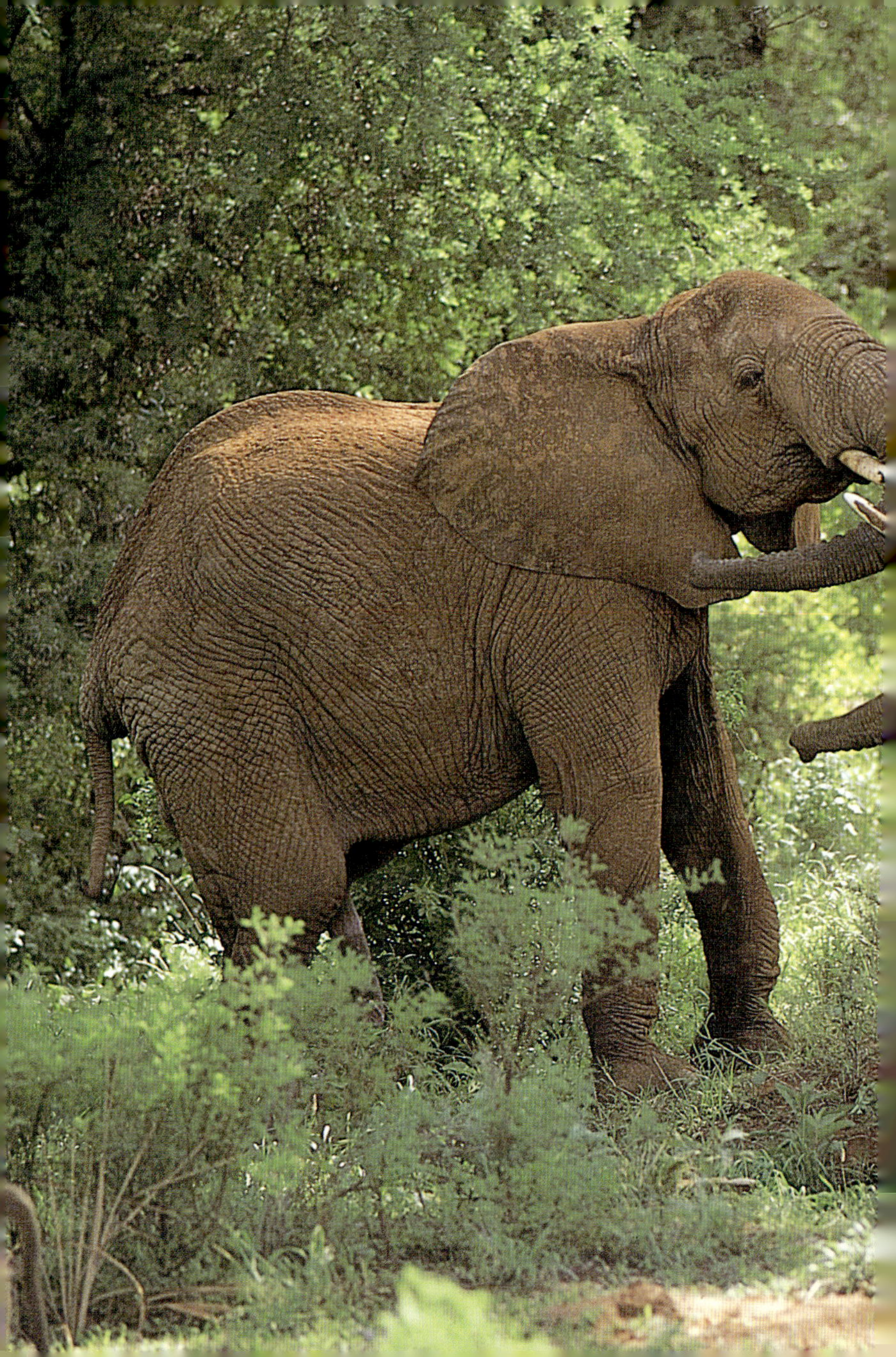

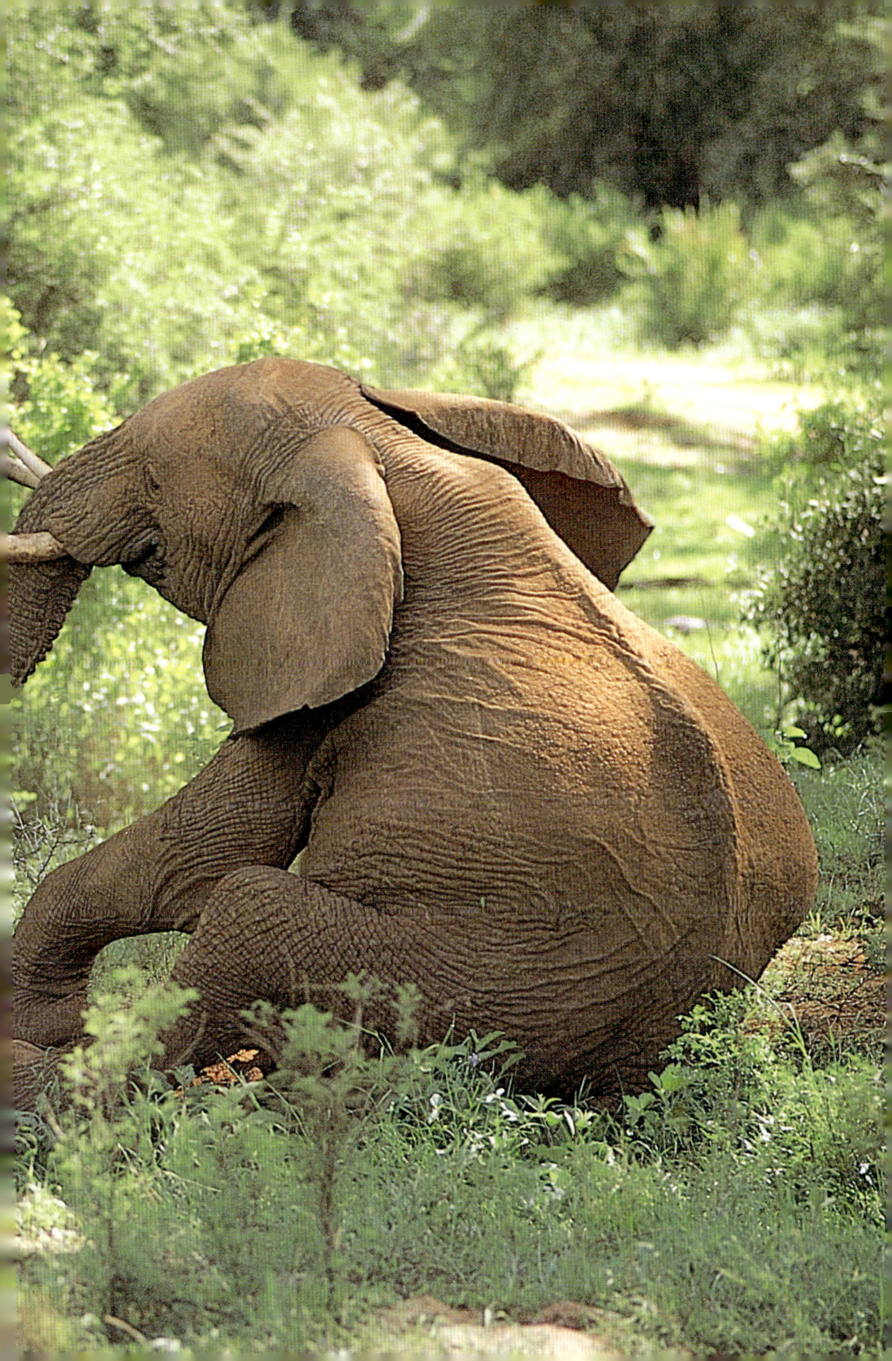

3. Samburu

Elephants, though by no means in their numbers of a hundred years ago, are seen frequently in the Samburu, Shaba and Buffalo Springs reserves but were almost exterminated in Shaba in the late 1970s after Kenya introduced the 1977 hunting ban. Before then poachers had been kept at bay.

For Arthur Neumann elephants were an obsession and, after he had hunted them all through these parts in 1894, life was never the same again. All Samburuland was open to him for his hunting safaris between 1894 and 1896 which coincided with the expeditions of Donaldson Smith.

A vast district still, of more than 20,000 square kilometres, extending north to the south-east shores of Lake Turkana and south to the Uaso Nyiro River, bounded on the west by Turkana and Pokot country and by Rendille country in the east, the Samburu National Reserve down in its south-east corner covers only a 165-square-kilometre fraction.

The reserve is bordered by ninety kilometres of the Uaso Nyiro River and it was beside it, close to where Samburu Lodge now stands, that Neumann made his camp. It is a beautiful spot, where the wide waters saunter down between banks on which *Acacia lahar* trees, the red thorn called *oltepesi* by the Maasai-Samburu people, give welcome shade. Neumann's camp was known, appropriately, as *Nyama yangu* — my meat — for there was usually plenty of elephant meat for his camp staff after he had removed the ivory.

Despite the Teutonic spelling of his name, Neumann was English. Born in Bedfordshire, England, in 1850, he was a shy and reticent man but became the friend of all the big game hunters of his day. Selous, Millais and Ward were among them and his book *Elephant Hunting in East Equatorial Africa* (Rowland Ward, 1897) — dedicated to his great friend MacLeod of MacLeod — is one of the epic hunting manuals of the last century.

Neumann had hunted in South Africa before arriving in Kenya in 1890, when he was one of a five-man party who made the first cross-country survey for a railway from the coast to Lake Victoria. British MPs dubbed it 'The Lunatic Line' but ultimately, after a shaky beginning, it became vital to Kenya's development. He was then involved with a second survey to find a better route. Only when that was completed in 1893 was he at last able to organise his first big elephant hunting safari.

His penetration of 'the interior' from Mombasa took him to the Mount Kenya region, across the Uaso Nyiro to the Lorogi Forest and then back to the Nyambenis, shooting record elephants and rhinos all the way.

Moving north to Lake Rudolf in 1895, he was wounded by an enraged elephant on New Year's Day 1896 and had to lie up for three months with badly crushed ribs. Finally he managed to struggle back to *Nyama yangu* to properly recuperate.

Shooting elephant, and making a living by trading their tusks at Mombasa, Neumann was besotted by the vast herds which he observed all through Samburuland. In his own words, he 'took damned little interest in shooting [any] other beast, but him [the elephant] I worship — I have become a true Ndorobo in that. Nothing else thrills me, but the spell of the elephant is as potent as ever.' He was assisted by Wandorobo hunters, for whom he had great respect and spoke their language. His guns were his .577 Gibbs, a double 10-bore Holland and Holland, a Mannlicher — 'for such trash as rhinos' as he put it — a .303 Lee Metford and a .450 Rigby.

With extreme reluctance, he had to end his activities when a big

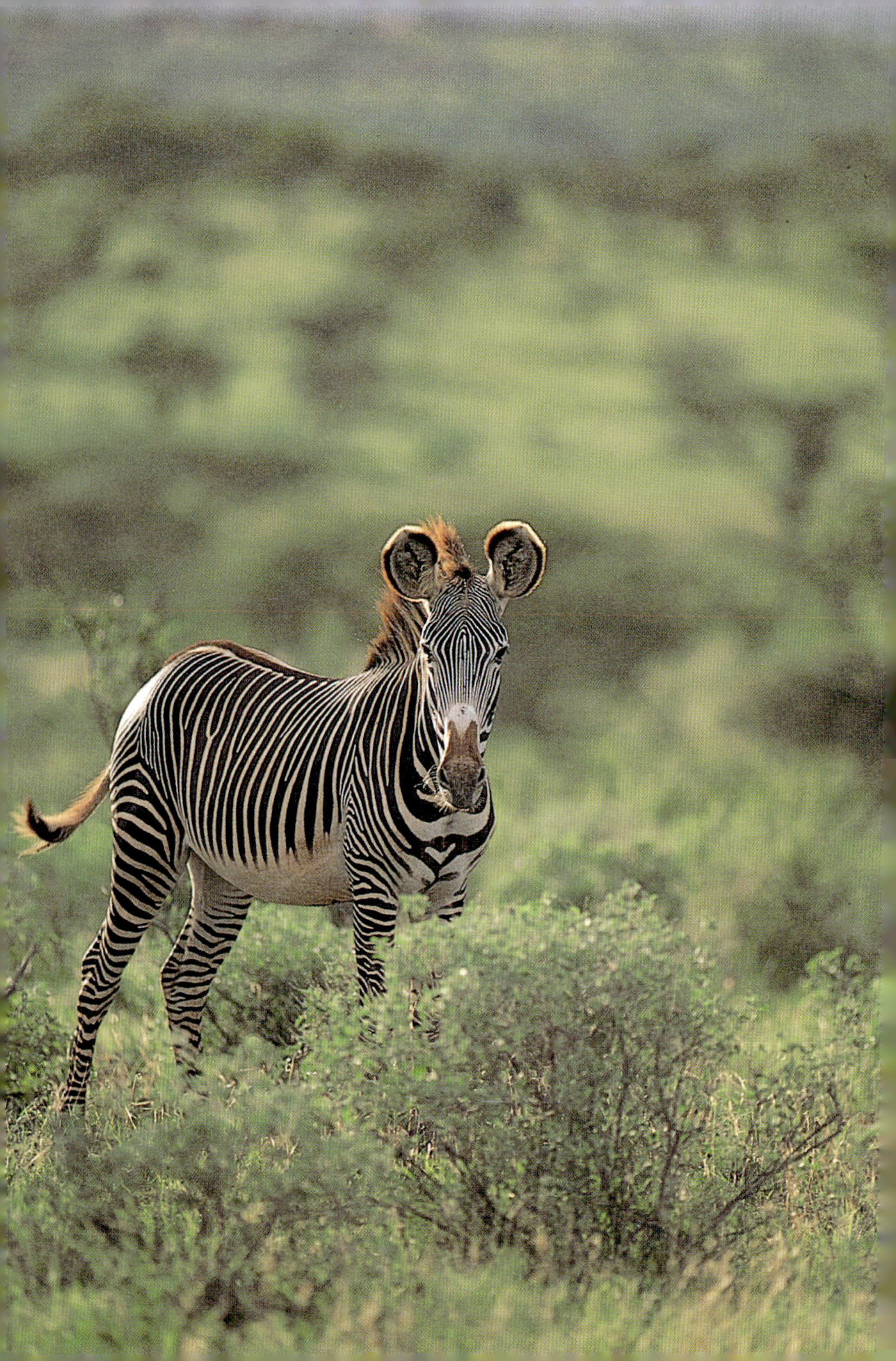

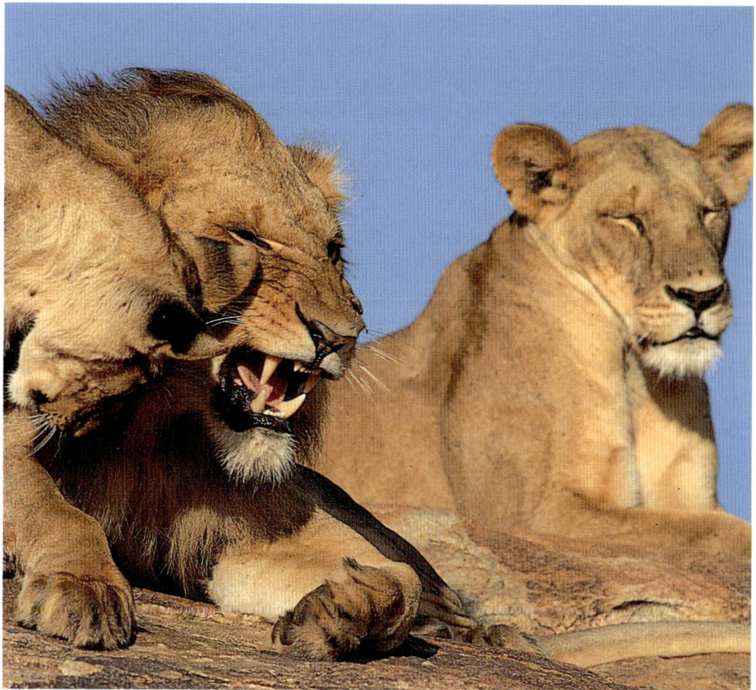

*Above: Lions (*Panthera leo*) the golden beasts of the golden lands. In Samburuland their coats and manes tend to be sparser than where there is more shade and cool.*

Right: Young impala — glossy-coated elegance despite the heat and dust.

Opposite: Grevy's zebra, so named because a gift of one was made to President Grevy of France in 1881 by the King of Shoa.

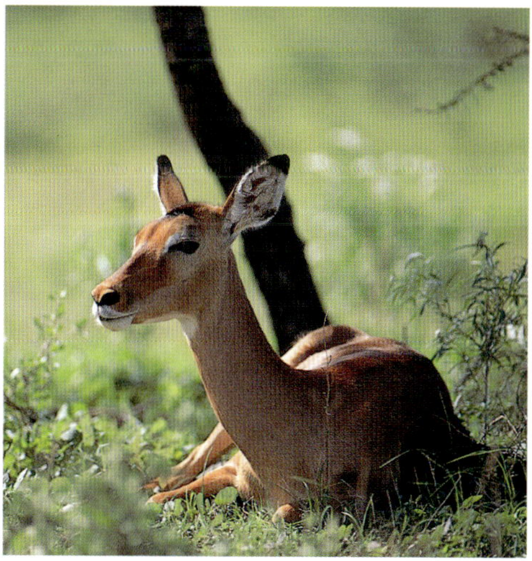

move toward game preservation took place in East Africa in 1905. While elephant hunting continued, it was in controlled hunting areas. Unaccustomed to restrictions of any kind, Neumann was utterly depressed by what looked like a finish to the life he loved.

He had always hunted on foot all over Samburuland, not least across Shaba's massive lava outcrops which he described in letters to his friend J G Millais:

'There is, between here and the Gwaso Nyiro River, a lot of lava country. The going is most cruel, especially when the grass covers the stones and it cuts one's boots to pieces in no time. There is one part where the ground is nothing but a mass of black, rough, broken lava debris. It forms low ridges and hillocks and is overgrown with scrubby bush, but is not very thick. There is little or no grass generally in this part. Here a herd of elephant often harbours. They are safe from the Ndorobos [Wandorobo] because they dare not tackle them here, as it is imposible to run away among the stones.'

He was right. It is not recommended to anyone lightly shod even to try it. Lacerated feet do not contribute to the enjoyment of any safari though there came medications in later years which to Neumann were unknown.

The outcrop which he described, north-west of the rolling Nyambeni Hills — another of his favourite hunting places — surges in a stark black groundmass to the east of the Nanyuki-Marsabit road, south of the Shaba reserve and between the road and the Mulbe River. It can be seen clearly from any vehicle entering the Samburu reserve by the Archer's Post gate, to the right of the road before crossing the Uaso Nyiro bridge. Neumann referred to the Nyambenis as 'the Jambeni range' when the 'J'

Overleaf: Less often seen than other big cats, the leopard will take its kill up into the branches of a tree to preserve what is not eaten immediately.

would have been pronounced like a 'Y' — 'Yambeni' — as people of many cultures still say 'Yambo' instead of 'Jambo', with a hard J.

Getting boots repaired in present-day Kenya is no problem, but to suffer serious damage to footwear a hundred years ago was little short of a disaster for Arthur Neumann — unless he had other pairs at his disposal, or was handy at doing the job himself. This he surely must have been. He was a past-master at self-sufficiency, stoically lying up in his small grass hut on the river bank, while savage injuries incurred during hunting forays healed themselves.

The 'furnishing' of his hut was primitive in the extreme, his bed made of branches cut from the surrounding trees and bushes; but for all its discomforts he was happy, enjoying what, to him, was more precious than anything else which life could offer — privacy and the right to do whatever he wanted whenever he chose. He would have found the lapping sounds of the Uaso Nyiro soothing, wide in these parts and scattered with sandbanks; and there was always the promise of excitement whenever he heard elephantine feet splashing through the shallows outside his hut.

Foreseeing the end of all this in 1905, he left Africa a deeply disappointed man.

Sad and lonely in England, where the traffic and the people confused him after years in the bush, his ears alert to every smallest sound, his only friends the Wandorobo, Samburu and Rendille people, his depression at the end must have been absolute. His ambition thwarted — to build himself a small house on the slopes of Mount Kenya in which to live out the rest of his days — he took his own life in 1907. For him, nothing could ever equal those golden Samburu days upon which, at the end, he must have looked back with longing and despair.

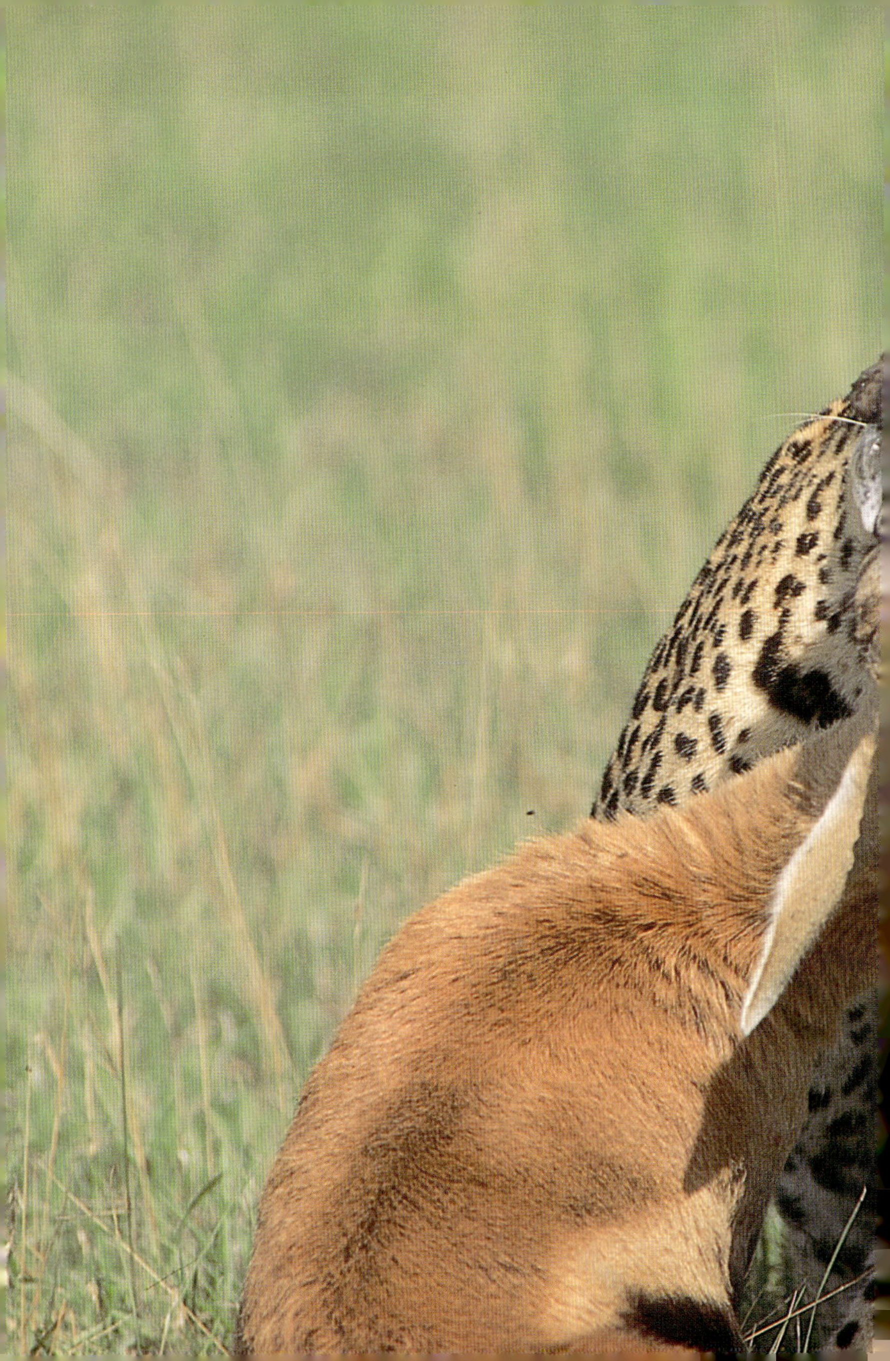

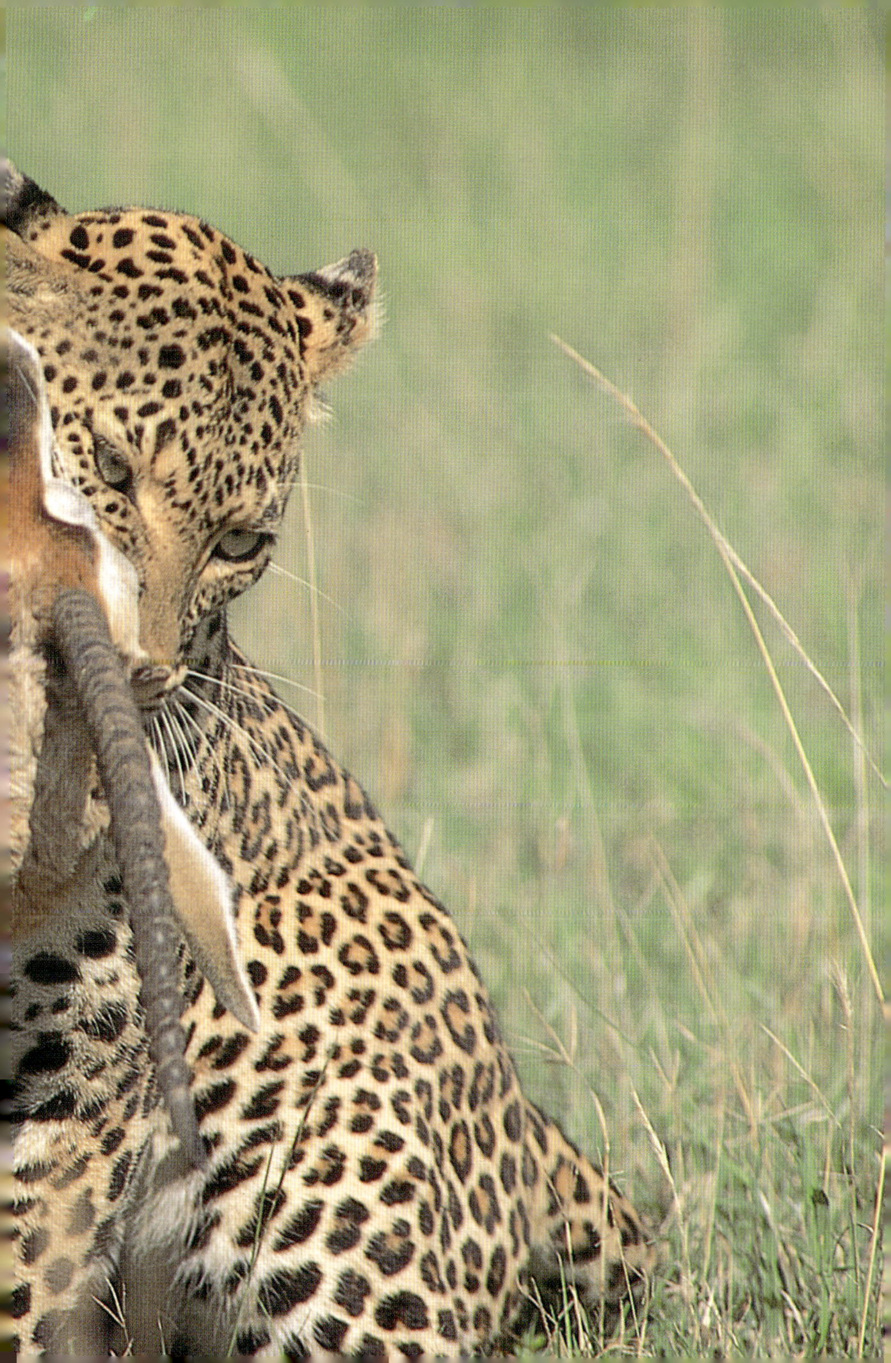

Neumann, one of the first Europeans to find heaven-on-earth in these golden lands, could never have had even the remotest inkling that thousands after him would share, though differently, the same lift of heart in being there. Scenically, at this end of the twentieth century, the Samburu reserve is one of the most exciting in Kenya, made the more enjoyable for the majority because the wildlife is no longer relentlessly plundered.

Rugged hills and mountains with magical names lie within the park and all around: Giltaman, Marti el Depe (Merti el Debi); Lowa Mara, Nashapa, Nakadeli, Koitogor (behind Larsen's Camp) and Lolkoitoi (to the west of Samburu Lodge and east of Samburu Intrepids). From them, seasonal streams and rivers flow down to the Uaso Nyiro: the Giltaman, Baa Lolgoto, Baa Lekoitogo, Lolkoitoi and Loga Lowa Mara.

Much of the year they are dried-up river beds which make driving in the park interesting — the soft sand of the *luggas* often patched and patterned by the spoor of a variety of large and small animals and scattered with a wealth of interesting stones: gneiss, limestone, quartz, lava, mica, asbestos and vermiculite which sparkle like gold and diamonds on the surface of the earth.

White, sun-bleached bones of nature's victims lie alongside. Were these creatures once peacefully drinking, perhaps, when there was water there, and predators snuffed out their lives to drag the flesh from their bones as the sun went down? Or were they drowned in some thundering torrent sweeping down the gully from the hillsides after rain, like sudden, powerful rivers in full spate?

Beyond the park and slightly to the south-west loom Ol Doinyo Lossos and Ol Doinyo Lolgurugi; to the north Ol Doinyo Sabachi, or Lololokwe as it is often called. Further north still lies the

Mathews Range — named by Teleki and von Höhnel as a tribute to the commander-in-chief of the Sultan of Zanzibar's army, General Lloyd Mathews, for the help he gave them in Zanzibar at the outset of their Lake Rudolf trip.

All are incredibly beautiful in the early morning and evening light, purple, green, blue and gold; but it is the closer, massive, flat-topped inselberg, the 1,853-metre-high bastion of Lololokwe which dominates the whole Samburu scene, visible from long distances around. In Samburuland, but outside the reserve, it offers an interesting challenge to mountain climbers as well as providing a directional landmark for anyone driving their own vehicle over unfamiliar ground in any of these three reserves.

The Samburu reserve, since 1948 part of the Great Northern Game Reserve which included Buffalo Springs and Shaba and extended north to Marsabit, was one of the earliest areas in Kenya to be set aside for wildlife conservation but attracted few visitors in the beginning because of its appalling access roads, too rugged for private vehicles. When the National Parks Administration, as it was then known, decided it could no longer afford to keep it going and proposed turning it over to grazing, conservationist and philanthopist Sir Malin Sorsbie offered to build a lodge there at his own expense, to make the park tourist-attractive and therefore self-supporting.

Samburu Lodge was opened officially on 13 July 1963 (now on long-lease from the Samburu County Council to the United Touring Company and managed by Block Hotels). Gifted outright by Sir Malin to the Samburu County Council to administer, it has become one of the best-loved tourist destinations in Kenya and has been extended several times since 1963.

Sir Malin later paid for an in-park bridge across the Uaso Nyiro

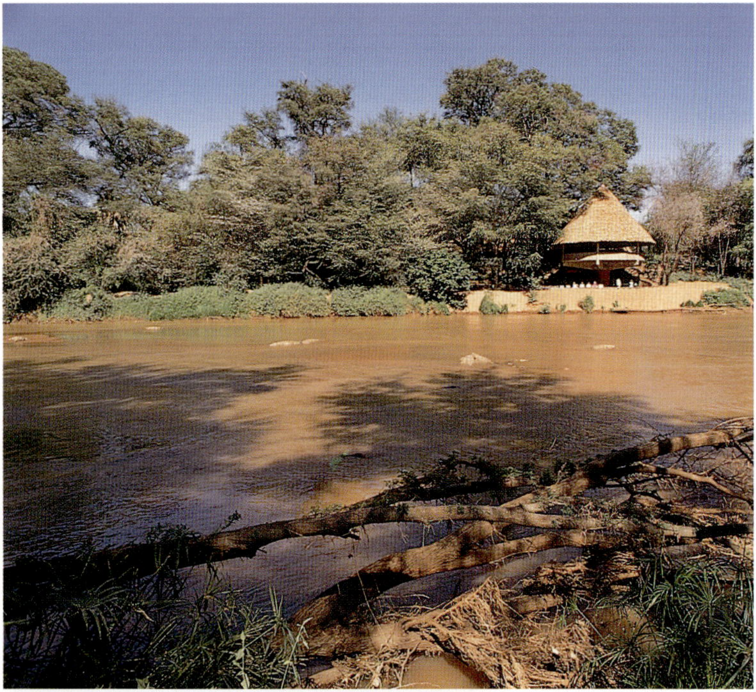

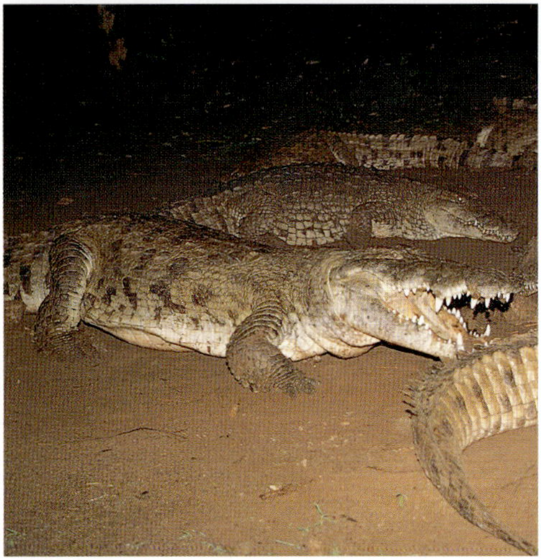

Above: Samburu Lodge from across the Uaso Nyiro River.

Left: Crocodiles can be watched in safety from the lodge's Crocodile Bar.

to give a shorter route to Buffalo Springs. Before then, visitors had to return to Archer's Post, cross the bridge there and pass through the Buffalo Springs (Chokaa) Gate. The bridge made a safari circuit through both parks possible, in each of which shady riverine drives give wildlife viewing at its best. From then on it became possible to explore, comfortably by vehicle, park roads and tracks which a hundred years ago Arthur Neumann would have had to hack his way through on foot. Unlike then, however, foot traffic is not allowed in any of the three reserves.

As tourism escalated, other in-park facilities on the north bank of the river followed Samburu Lodge: Samburu Intrepids Club in the western sector of the reserve not far from the park's West Gate, and Larsen's Camp.

The roadside settlement of Archer's Post has been known by that name ever since Geoffrey Francis Archer, as District Commissioner in 1909 for the vast Northern Frontier Province, sited his base depot on the north side of the river. The slow collection of dusty but colourful *dukas* (shops), houses, police post, filling station, school and mission hospital has been taking place for eighty years.

An impressive, two-metre-tall figure, later knighted for his skills and bravery, Archer — a nephew of Sir Frederick Jackson — was a keen ornithologist and big game sportsman and the author of *Birds of British Somaliland* and, as a record of the times, *Memoirs of an East African Administrator* (1963).

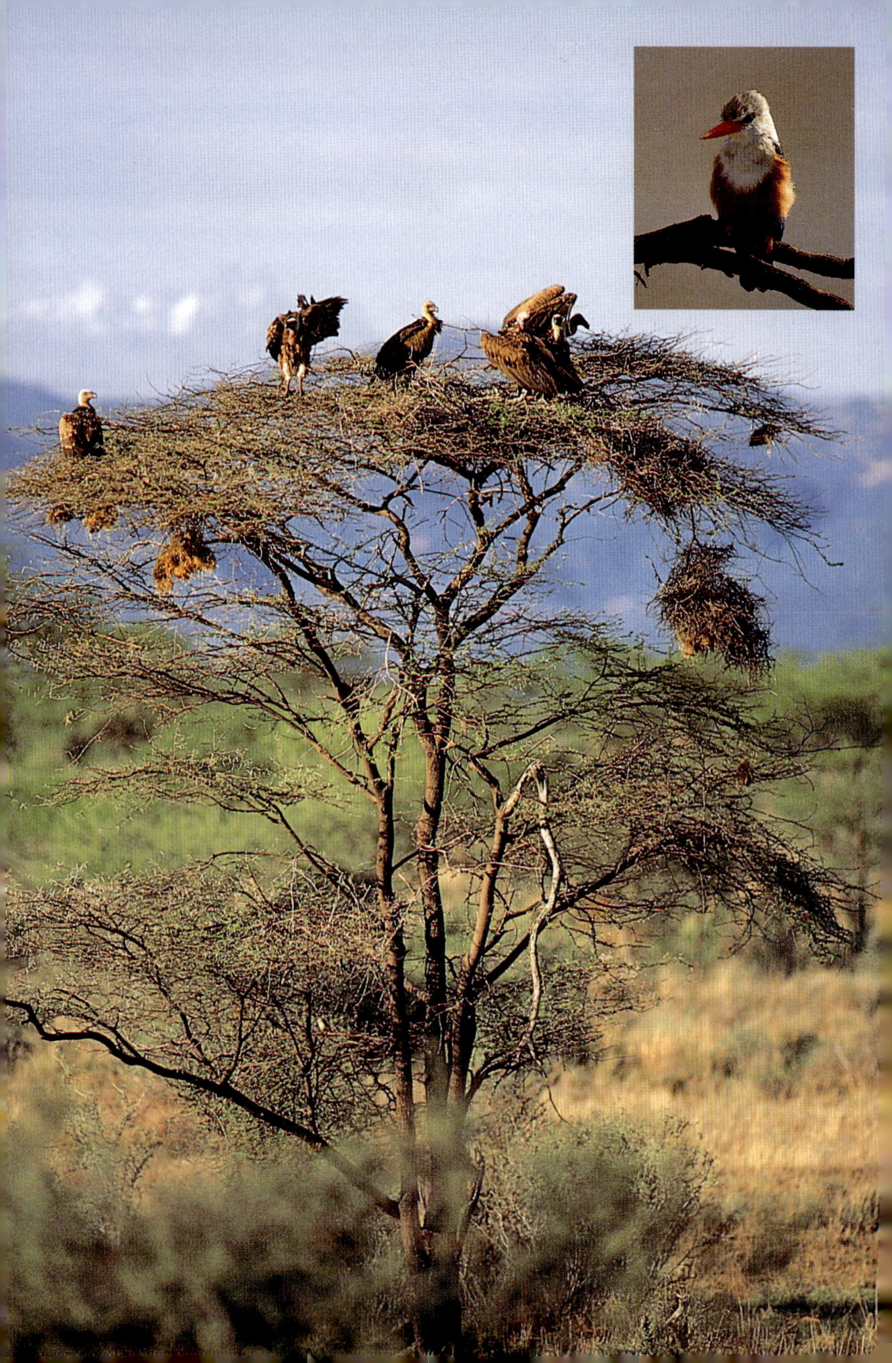

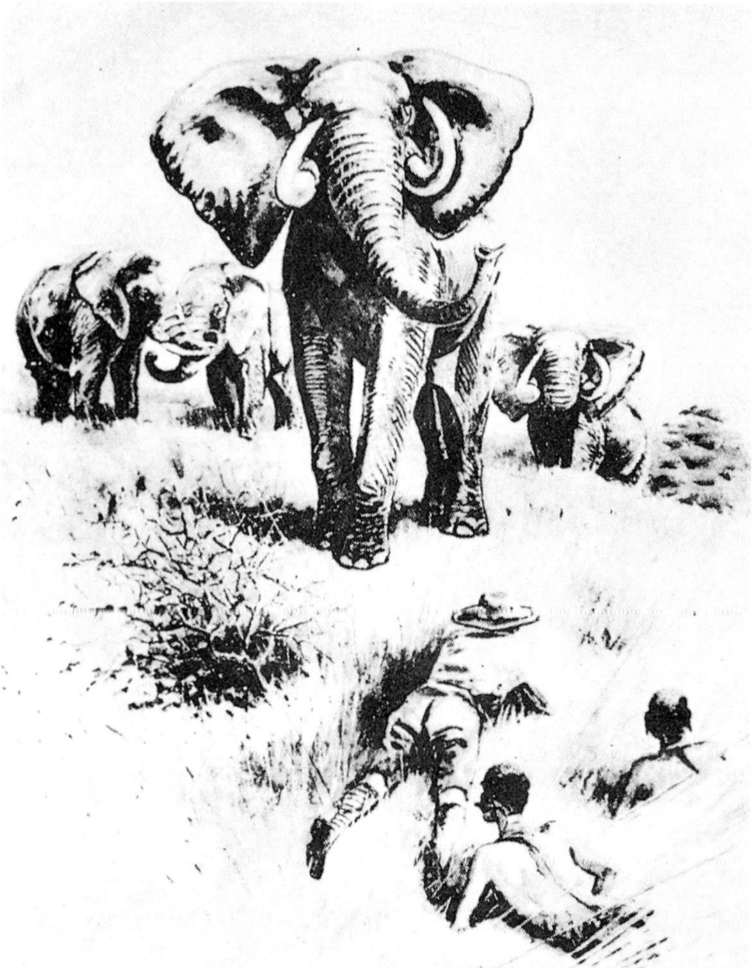

*Opposite top: Malachite Kingfisher (*Alcedo christata*).*

Opposite: Ever present vultures in the golden land await carrion upon which to feed.

Above: The artist J G Millais' picture from his Wanderings and Memories *(1919) of Arthur Neumann on an elephant hunt.*

4. Buffalo Springs

One of the great surprises of Kenya's National Parks and Reserves, since there are so many of them, is that no two are really alike. Buffalo Springs and Samburu are contiguous and are often treated as one unit, both commanding a common stretch of the Uaso Nyiro River, but they are administered by two separate county councils. Samburu is run from the Samburu District headquarters at Maralal in Kenya's Rift Valley Province. Buffalo Springs and Shaba are controlled by the Isiolo District headquarters at Isiolo in the country's Eastern Province.

Each beautiful in its own, sometimes stark, very African way, the two parks are different in terrain. Beyond the level stretches adjacent to the Uaso Nyiro, Samburu is scattered with hills, mountains and many dried-up beds of seasonal streams and rivers forded by concrete drifts. Buffalo Springs, apart from its green, wooded, riverine frontage, is — by way of contrast — a stretch of wide, silver-sanded flatlands extending southwards from the river to the Ngare Mara Gate in the reserve's south-east corner and beyond the park border almost to Isiolo. A map-like perspective is offered from the Kubi Panya Lookout Point on higher ground west of the Ngare Mara Gate.

This is a reserve of uncluttered distances, of termite mounds of architectural proportions in all shapes and sizes and of sandy, lowland plains over which frisky dust-devils sometimes seem as if they are the only visible signs of activity in the midday heat which shimmers like a mirage over the quivering land. The Isiolo, Keromet, Maji ya Chumvi (which translates from Kiswahili to 'Salt Water') and Ngare Mara rivers flow from south to north into the Uaso Nyiro.

Easiest access to the springs and their surrounding swamps is from the main park road from the Buffalo Springs Chokaa Gate on the A2 Isiolo-Archer's Post-Marsabit road in the east, where a riverwards secondary circuit leads to the springs and then back again onto the main track. Roughly speaking, the springs bubble up about half-way between the gate and Buffalo Springs Lodge.

The reserve is almost entirely without signposts (except for the lodge) and it is easy to lose one's way even with a park map, for many of the roads are crossed by unmarked tracks or fork into two almost identical sandy branches in a manner which is quite bewildering.

A keen sense of direction is a great advantage and an ability to see and remember recognisable landmarks, such as the great mass of Lololokwe beyond Samburu to the north, or the green river line. If the absence of signposts does nothing else, it at least sharpens the sense of adventure and, somewhat disconcertingly sometimes, confirms that there are still many places in Kenya where — not always from choice — one is out on one's own.

The river section of the reserve which, gamewise, is usually the most rewarding, extends from Samburu Serena Lodge in the west (despite its name it is on the south side of the river) to the reserve's eastern boundary on the A2. The riverside park track covers only half of this distance, from Samburu Serena to the Buffalo Springs Lodge.

Many of the larger animals cross the river frequently from one side to the other, particularly elephant and buffalo. Their advantage in doing so is not always obvious. A herd observed in the morning happily grazing in Samburu, may be seen crossing the river into Buffalo Springs in the late afternoon. Buffalo may be in herds of fifty or more. Both species wade across the crocodile-infested shallows to occupy either park as home. There are often casualties. Oryx, Grevy zebra, common zebra, gerenuk and giraffes — both the Maasai giraffe and the reticulated — tend to remain within the park in which

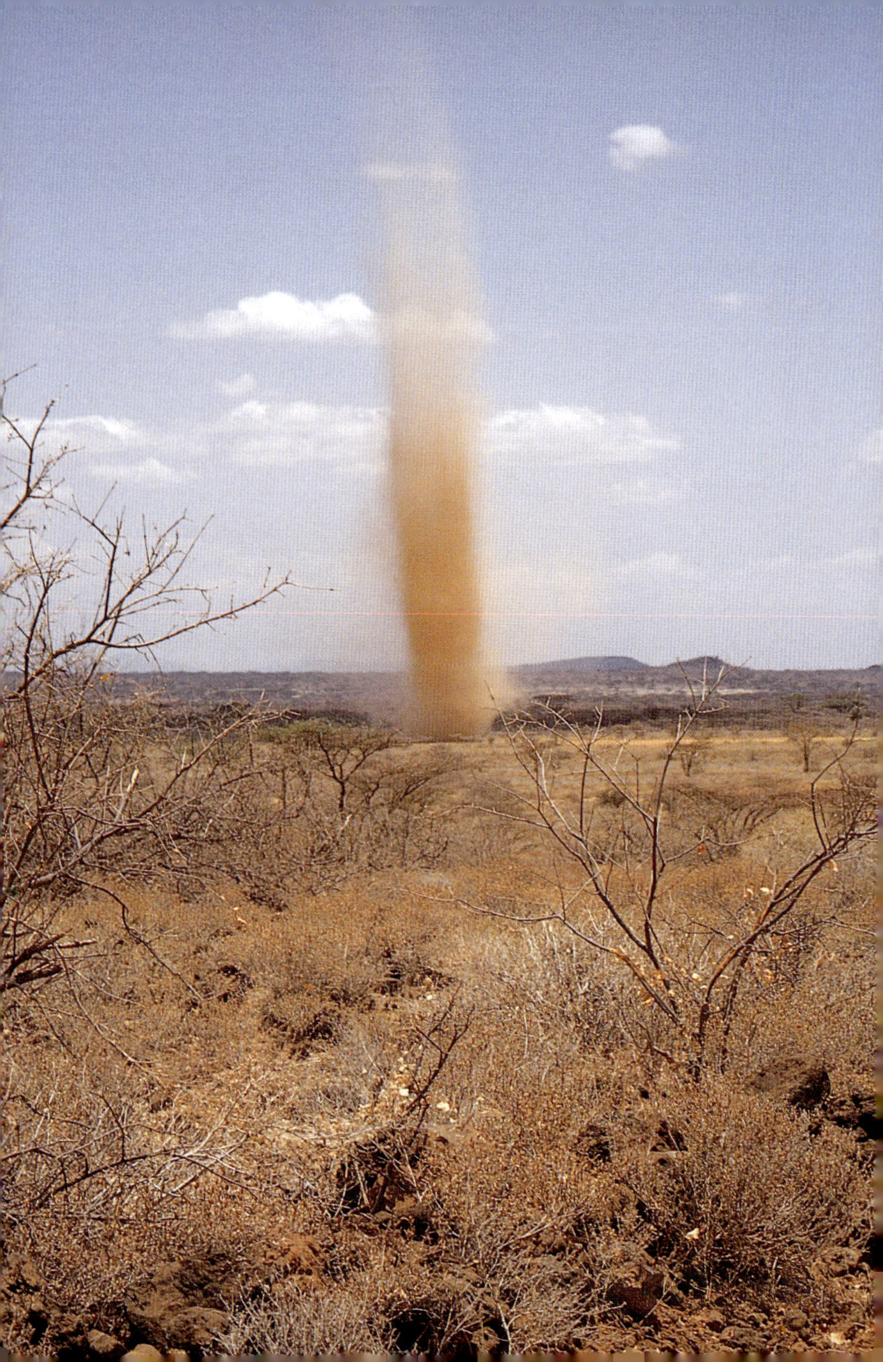

Opposite: Buffalo Springs, where the hot inland winds set dust devils whirling across the barren land. Overleaf: The brown river turns crimson with the dying day.

they were probably born. All are common to both reserves.

The predators do not always find it easy to cross the river unless the water is very low, but they sometimes manage it and will be found wherever the plains game are concentrated. Lion can swim and do. Cheetah are often seen on the Buffalo Springs side of the water, lying in wait, stalking their prey and making the final kill.

On the rare occasions after heavy rain in the areas upstream, when it is impossible for the animals to cross, any caught unawares are doomed. With a roar like that of a powerful steam engine, a great tidal wave bears down from the west, carrying with it whole uprooted trees, other heavyweight debris and the bodies of drowned wild and domestic animals. The water between the two parks rises three metres or more with ferocious suddenness and, overnight, drops back again to its average level.

The springs, three kilometres from Buffalo Springs Lodge and the focal point in the park for both animals and people, were sporadically bombed by the Italians based in Abyssinia (now Ethiopia) at the beginning of the 1939-45 war. The airmen thought that 'in the centre of Kenya' they must be over Nairobi.

Of the two pools at the springs, each fed by the melt waters of Mount Kenya, one is a swimming pool. The other reed-fringed pool is a watering place for the wildlife, who use it for drinking, bathing and wallowing. If in appearance the former is the less attractive of the two, it is because the protection wall surrounding it became essential to keep the elephants, buffalos, hippos and crocodiles out. Fairly for all, the animals' watering place is out-of-bounds as a swimming pool for humans.

Whatever is read about them, or seen on film, crocodile are dangerous and are to be viewed and photographed with extreme

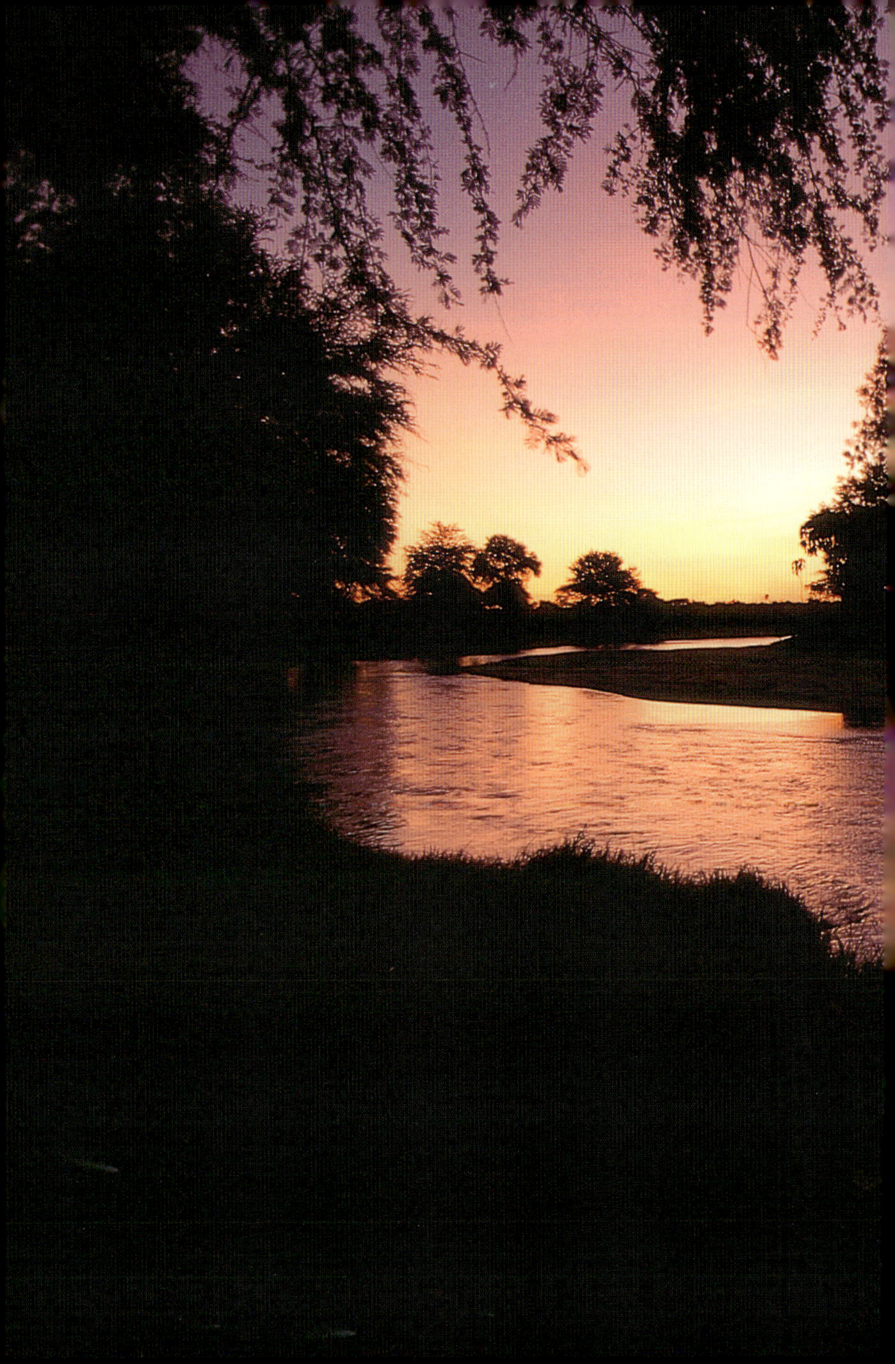

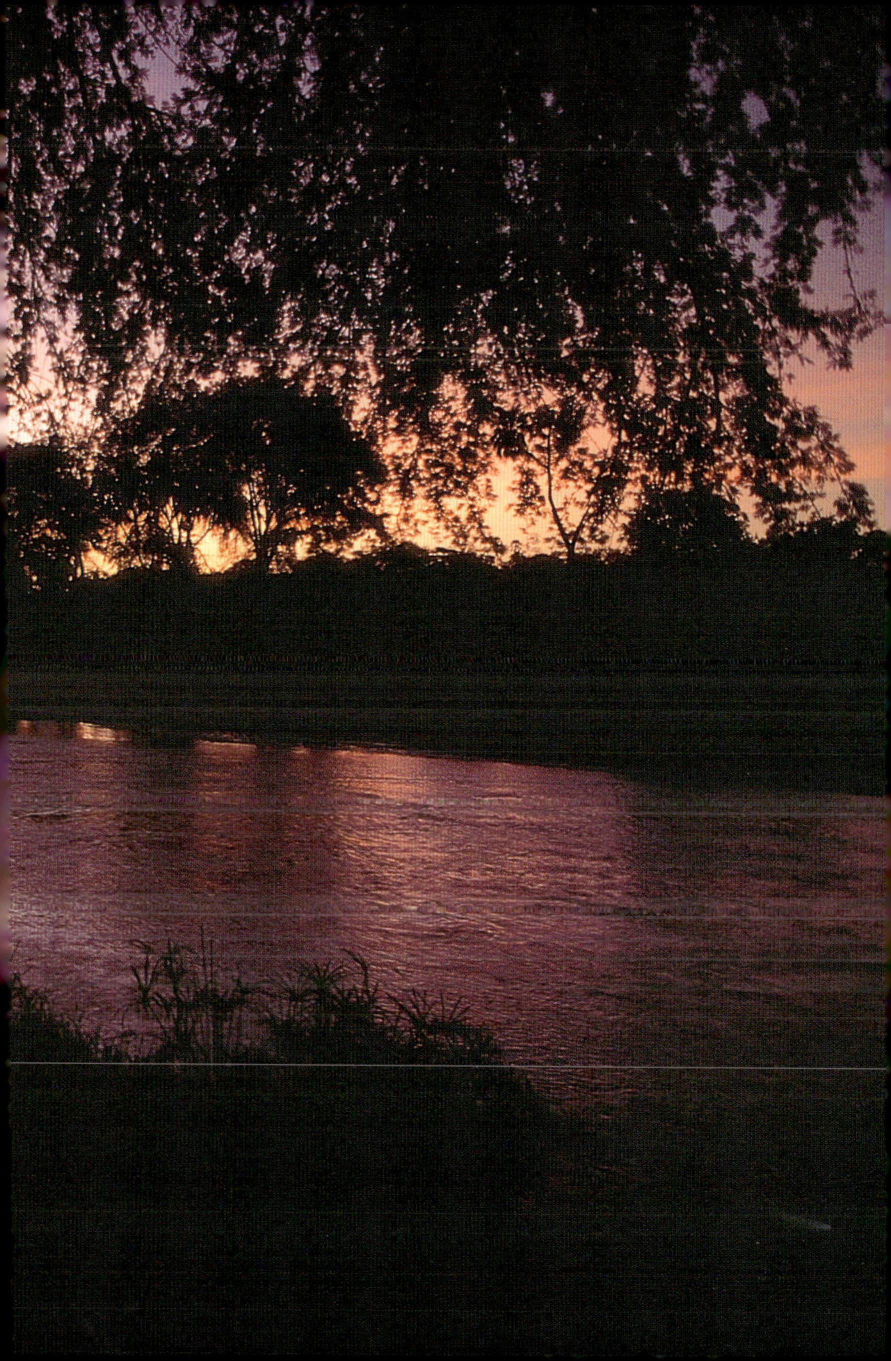

caution. An eyeball-to-eyeball encounter with one in a river or pool is confrontation with a hideous death, and hippo have not been unknown to snap a man in half between their powerful jaws.

There can be no such thing in a wildlife reserve as humans and animals sharing the same drinking and bathing facilities. For visitors to Buffalo Springs, however, it is rather splendid to know, ninety kilometres from the 5,199–metre summit of Mount Kenya, in a climate that rarely falls below 26°C in the shade and remains the same day and night, that in the pool they can cool off in the melted snows of Africa's second highest mountain, once believed to be the location of the legendary King Solomon's Mines.

If celebrating your visit with a glass — or two — of champagne on the top of Champagne Ridge appeals, there's nothing against it providing you have brought your own, for there's no 'corner shop' in this or the other two reserves. Legend has it that you would only be paying your respects to a tradition set, in 1909, by an ex-president of the USA, Theodore 'Teddy' Roosevelt, who camped there beneath spreading acacia trees while on his historic hunting safari. He and his son Kermit were collecting specimens for the Smithsonian Institute and for most of the expedition, either singly or together, were accompanied by some of the most experienced professional guides of the day.

Father and son each celebrated their birthdays while 'on safari' — 'Teddy' his fifty-first and Kermit his twentieth.

'One of the troubles of hunting as a naturalist', the big man was to write in his epic *African Game Trails* (1910), 'is that it necessitates the presence of a long tail of men to take off and carry in the big skins, in order that they may ultimately appear in museums.' But, as most world media had reported with delight at the time, when the safari

Overleaf: Samburu ostrich and young, all too often prey to predators.

started out from the front of Nairobi's Norfolk Hotel, headed by the Roosevelts, it included their several professional guides and their assistants, gunbearers, trackers, skinners, cooks, camp staff and 'five hundred porters each carrying a twenty-kilo headload comprising everything from collapsible baths to cases of champagne.'

For his Uaso Nyiro interlude, however, 'Teddy' was accompanied only by the hunter R J Cuninghame — Kermit had gone off to Baringo with the hunter Leslie Tarlton — and the minimum of gunbearers, skinners and staff needed to maintain their several camps. They marched from Nyeri in the foothills of Mount Kenya, encountering a rather different type of wildlife on the way, 'ants on safari, just as we were', and shot eland 'along the edge of a big swamp. Hardly had we skinned the carcass before the vultures lit on it.' Roosevelt recorded that his gunbearer, Bakhari, coming across a cock and hen ostrich with chicks cried out: 'Look, sah! Ostrich bull, cow and pups!' The whole company found ostrich meat deliciously edible.

They saw the plains beside the Uaso Nyiro 'crawling with [common] zebra. In every direction there were herds of scores or of hundreds'.

Each morning they were up at dawn 'and saw the heavens redden and the sun flame over the rim of the world. All day long we rode and walked across the endless flats, save at noon, when the sky was like molten brass, we might rest under the thin half-shade of some thorn tree. As the shadows lengthened and the harsh, pitiless glare softened, we might turn campwards, or we might hunt until the sun went down and the mountains in the far-off west, and the sky above them, grew faint and dim . . . then we would ride back through the soft, warm beauty of the tropic night, the stars blazing overhead and the silver moonlight flooding the reaches of dry grass; it was so bright that our

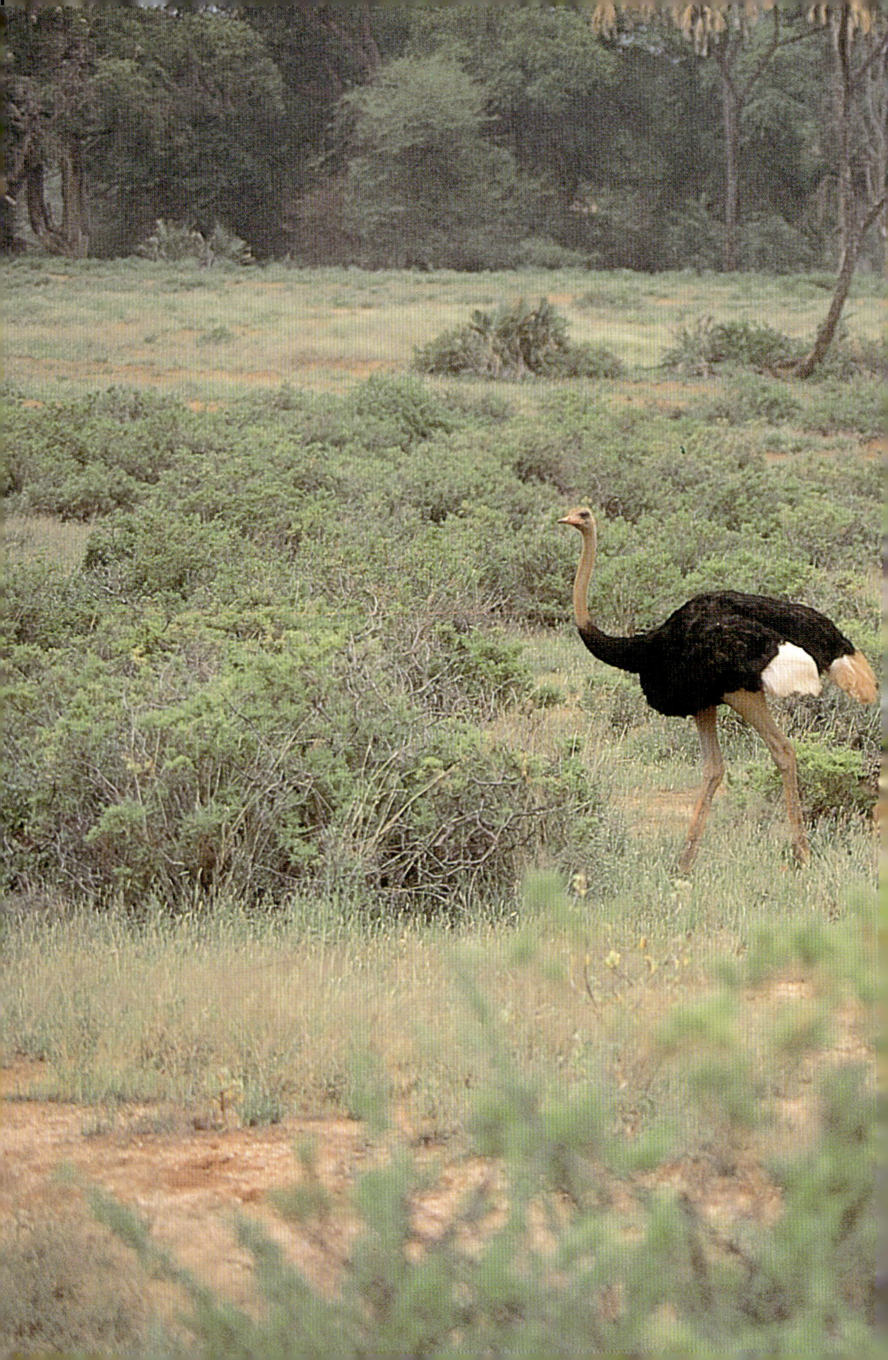

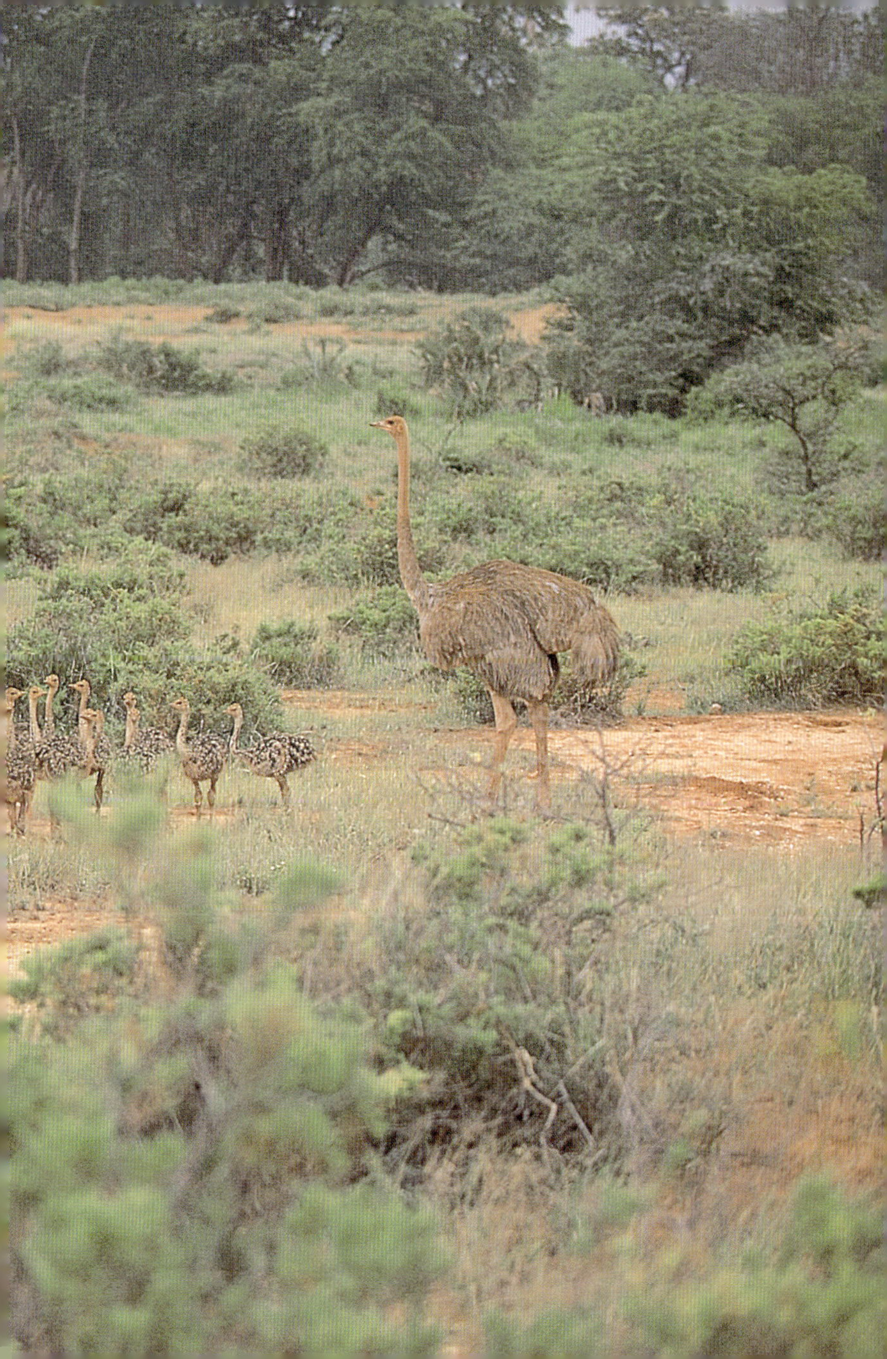

shadows were almost as black and as clearcut as in the day.'

Never a man to despise water wherever it was found when on safari, 'Teddy' usually took the precaution of seeing that his porters — or the donkeys — were humping a case or more of champagne. He was later to write in *African Game Trails*, in which he devoted a whole chapter to his hunting adventures along the 'Guaso Nyero', that 'the water was foul, but in a dry country one grows gratefully to accept as water anything that is wet.' How much more grateful he must have been, returning to camp on Champagne Ridge after a long, hot, tiring, foot-blistering day, to find a glass or two of the sparkling grape awaiting him. It was probably lukewarm (how otherwise?) but double satisfaction must have been his, nonetheless, knowing that with each bottle down the hatch he was reducing the porters' carrying load for the next day.

The dictionary description of 'champaign' is hardly applicable to this particular park ridge: 'Flat and open ground; a clear level landscape; a broad treeless plain', for the Roosevelt party was already up on the higher land which was by no means treeless and it was the view they looked down upon, rather than the ridge itself, which would have been the 'champaign'. As far as Kenya was concerned, the Roosevelt safari was 'The Safari of the Year', if not of the decade, and their adventures described in *African Game Trails* made exciting reading for armchair explorers everywhere. The collection with which the expedition returned was of birds as well as mammals, and recent reports reveal that keen birdwatchers and ornithologists may expect to see well over 300 different species in the Buffalo Springs reserve.

More often associated in their latter years with Shaba (Joy) and Kora (George) it was the Adamsons who set up camp in 1963 on the site now occupied by Buffalo Springs Lodge. The park was their home when George, as game warden for the area since 1961, undertook to make a game count — a fairly lengthy exercise. He and Joy then built themselves a rondavel to replace the tents which, up until then, had sufficed. They called the rondavel *Ndovu* (Elephant) and it proved so popular with visitors that they built three more, calling them *Duma* (Cheetah), *Nyati* (Buffalo) and *Mamba* (Crocodile).

This modest self-help visitor accommodation in the park, initiated by the Adamsons, became the basis of the first Buffalo Springs Tented Camp (now the 92-bed Buffalo Springs Lodge) and the Adamsons moved away from Buffalo Springs to their next camp at Shaba.

Only fractionally north of the equator, with an area of 128 square kilometres, Buffalo Springs National Reserve is the smallest of the three-park complex, only slightly more than half the size of Shaba. The altitudes in the park range from 792 to 975 metres above sea level.

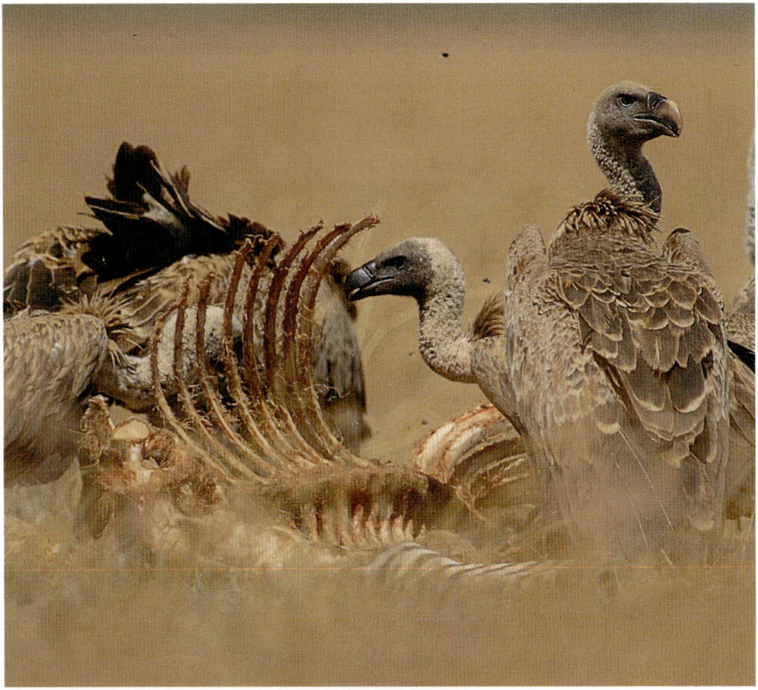

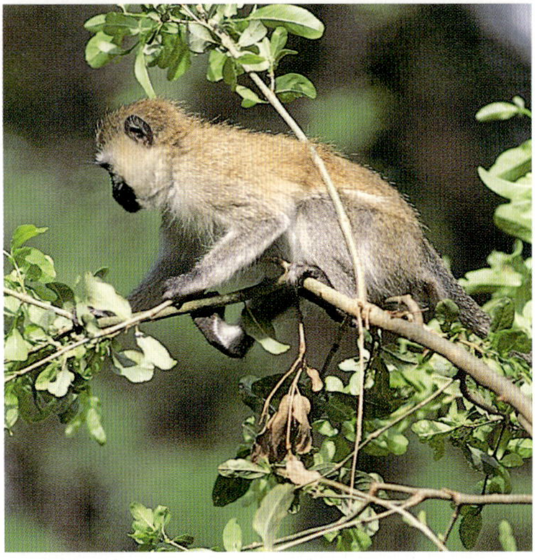

Above: White-backed vultures (Pseudogyps africanus) *on kill.*

Left: Vervet monkey (Cercopithecus aethiops) *gregarious, arboreal and terrestrial.*

Opposite top: Grevy's zebra are grazers but, where grass is scant, they will eat any other foliage they can find.

Opposite: When the streams and rivers dry up, a mudbath is the next best thing.

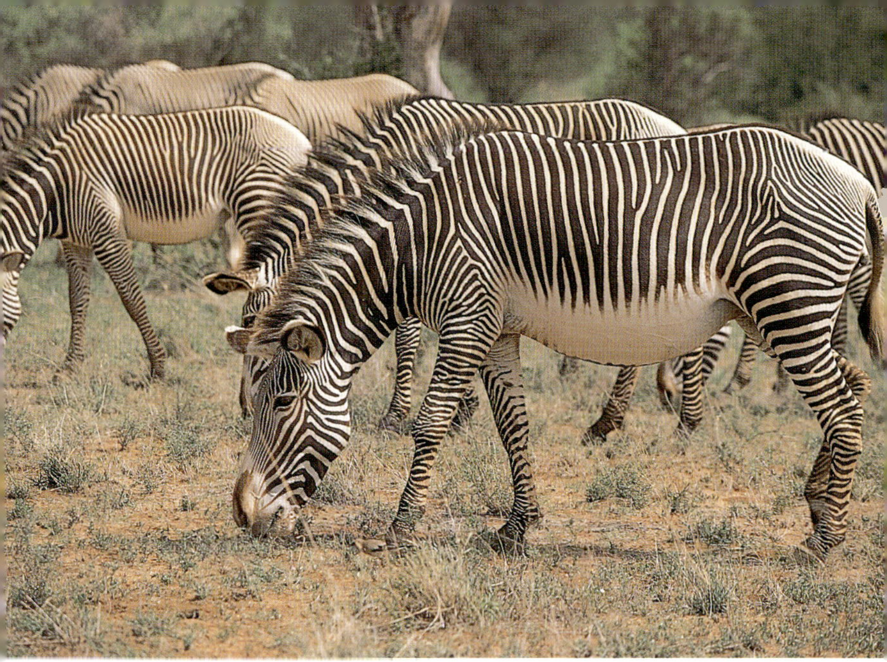

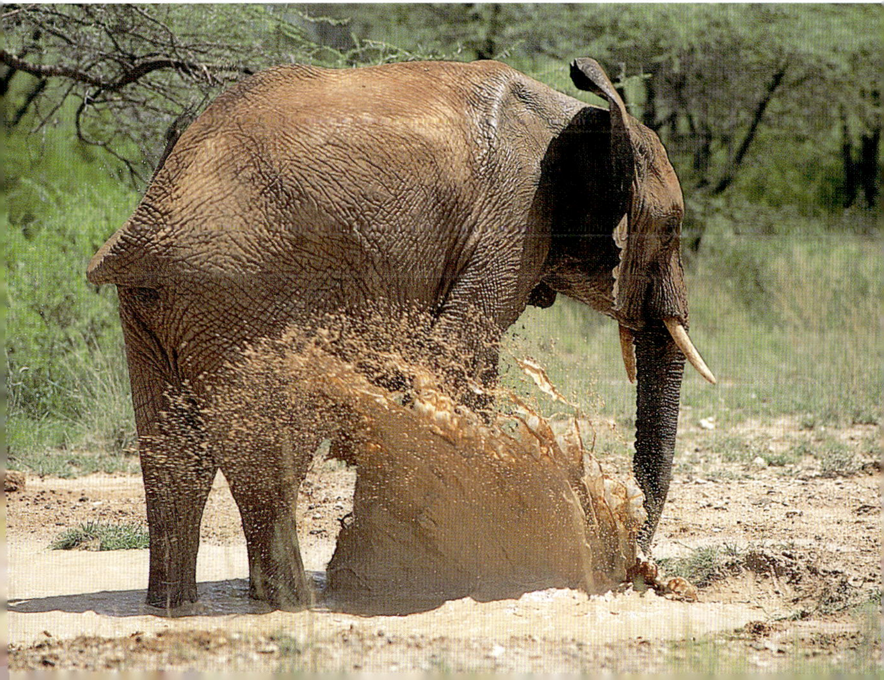

5. Shaba

With its uncluttered plains bordering on the river, Shaba, an area of 239 square kilometres, is the most noticeably golden of this three-park complex, except when welcome rains briefly carpet the flatlands with sudden emerald green. It is the largest of the three reserves.

Unlike Samburu with its many hills, dried-up river beds and surrounding mountains, Shaba is mostly spacious, level, sandy country, of great appeal to all who love 'the *bundu*' — the semi-arid bush country or natural, unspoiled Africa. More often than not it is a case of love at first sight. Tourist minibuses are not seen nearly so frequently there as in Samburu and Buffalo Springs and the only development in the park, apart from its three gates, is riverside Sarova Shaba Lodge quite close to the Natorbe Gate, the most frequent point of entry.

From inside Shaba, all the lands north of the Uaso Nyiro are outside the reserve but red, rugged Bodich immediately north of the river — rising 1,443 metres from the plains — is conspicuous from almost all quarters of the park, the source of many of the tributaries feeding the Uaso Nyiro from the north, including the Larisoro. It gives a dramatic backdrop for photographs of the animals — the oryx, waterbuck and plains game which tend to congregate near the water; and where there are plains game there are predators. There are many worse ways of spending a day in Shaba than by taking a picnic lunch to the river which is wide there and quite fast-flowing over large mid-stream stones and sandbanks.

A scenic riverside drive may be made from the extreme north-west of the reserve to the Sharinka Falls and Gafarsa Gate in the north-east, making animal study and photography irresistible all along the way. Shaba's river frontage extends for some thirty-four kilometres.

Directly south of Bodich, the Shaba massif is another striking landmark, a strangely shaped volcanic cone from which lava once poured out across a huge area, leaving places still barely covered with any vegetation. At a height of 1,623 metres, its main bulk lies outside the reserve and, looking back at it from the north, very much resembles a giant tortoise with raised head — as if in pain — or a crouching rabbit without ears. A pleasant, sandy, southern circuit road to the pretty self-help Funan Camp Site, Shaba Gate and the remains of Joy Adamson's one-time camp passes by its lower slopes which extend into the park. Shaba Dogo (little Shaba), also called Shaptiga, lies further south still, at a lesser 1,290 metres.

Because of the privacy it afforded, Shaba was the golden country chosen by the artist, author and student of animal behaviour Joy Adamson when conducting her leopard rehabilitation work and it is now sad history that she was murdered there in January 1980, only a few metres from her camp in front of one of the several swamps which come as such a surprise in these otherwise barren lands. The murder spot is so close to the camp that the mystery still remains how no-one heard her call out or — if hearing — did not go to investigate.

Since her death, the scene from where her tree-shaded tent once stood is towards a reed-fringed lake where herdsmen water their goats, sheep and cattle — the sturdy, hump-backed Boran cattle, more disease-resistant than any other species in East Africa. Camels and donkeys saunter down to the edges to join them where, in the sheer delight and luxury of cool, cleansing water in the savage heat of a sun-baked, dusty Shaba day, young boys play and splash about and call across to each other and tall, slender women come down to fill their pots and gourds.

All this activity Joy would not have tolerated, for total privacy was

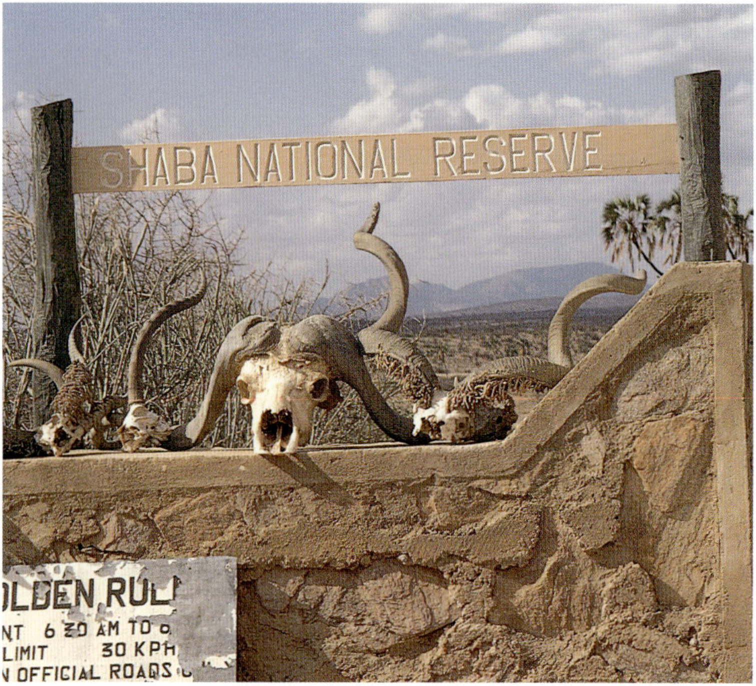
SHABA NATIONAL RESERVE
OLDEN RUL
NT 6 30 AM TO
LIMIT 30 KPH
N OFFICIAL ROADS

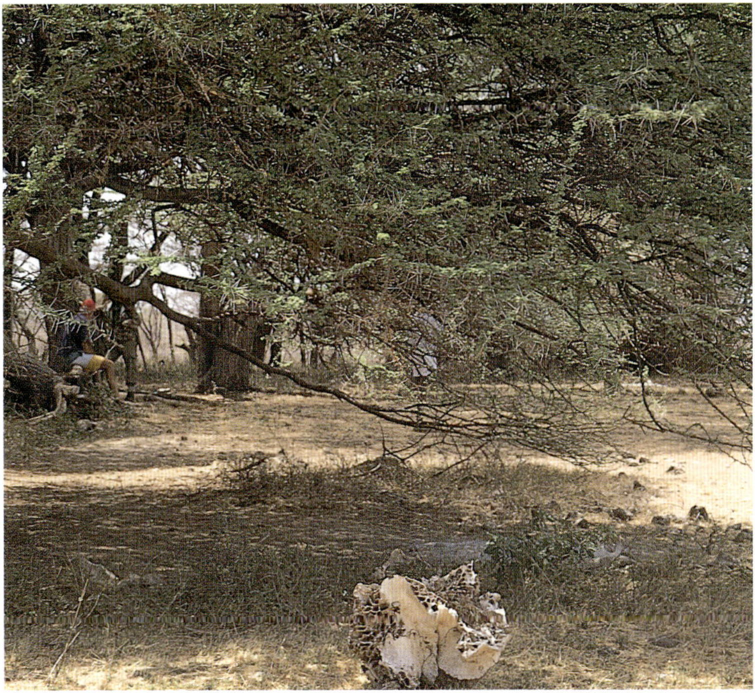

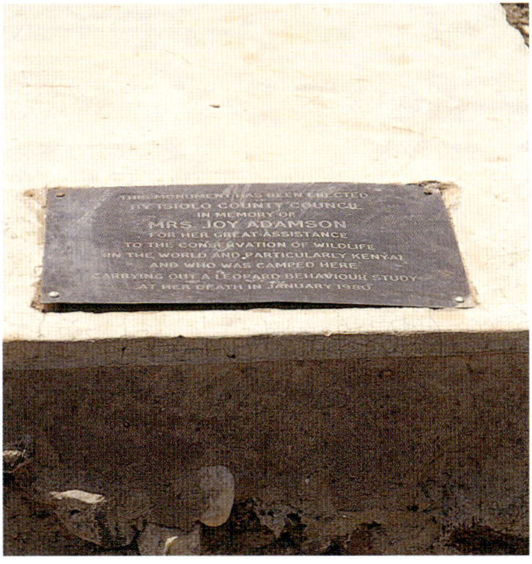

Above: Acacias shade Joy Adamson's one-time campsite, where the bleached skulls and bones of pachyderms still lie about.

Right: A bronze plaque on a stone plinth marks the spot where Joy Adamson was murdered in January 1980.

Opposite: The Natorbe Gate is the most-used entrance to the Shaba National Reserve.

what she sought in Shaba, in order to carry out her studies on her beloved leopard, Penny. She was in the process of writing *Penny, Queen of Shaba* when she died.

For the visitor in more recent years, however, the view from the old camp site presents a living picture to capture any artist's eye, the bright sunlight, the people, the animals and the women's colourful, ankle-length garments clinging wetly to their legs.

Of Joy's camp beneath the large acacia trees, only a few wooden posts remain to show where it once stood, roughly bordered by rocks random-daubed with white (as a guideline back to the camp after dark but along which, one late evening at dusk, she never returned). The bleached skulls of some long-dead pachyderms and herbivores lie about.

The murder spot is marked by a stone plinth bearing an engraved plate, erected by the Isiolo County Council, as a tribute to her all too abruptly-ended life and work:

This monument has been erected
by Isiolo County Council
in memory of
Mrs Joy Adamson
for her great assistance
to the conservation of wildlife
in the world and particularly in Kenya
and who was camped here
carrying out a leopard behaviour study
at her death in January 1980

*Overleaf: Tawny eagles (*Aquila rapax*) mating. Their plumage can vary greatly from pale to dark brown.*

Known best internationally for her three books about the lioness Elsa, *Born Free, Living Free* and *Forever Free* — much read and more than once filmed — which were followed by *The Spotted Sphinx, Pippa the Cheetah, The Peoples of Kenya, Joy Adamson's Africa* and her autobiography *The Searching Spirit* (1978), Joy is remembered in Kenya, more perhaps than elsewhere, for her meticulous botanical paintings and those of the country's tribes and sub-tribes in their traditional costumes and ornamentation. Many of them were done during her travels with her second husband, the botanist and curator of Nairobi Museum, Peter Bally. Others were done after her third and last marriage — in 1944 — to George Adamson, 'Bwana Game'.

It was on her first safari with George to Samburuland that Joy became too ill to paint the Samburu people, but she resolved to return and her paintings of the tribes of the (then) Northern Frontier District, now hang in the Nairobi Museum. They include the Samburu, Boran, Rendille, Maasai, Turkana, Gabra, Galla and El Molo people.

Articulate in her painting and writing, and in her often impassioned monologues when it was just about impossible for anyone else to get a word in edgeways, she found tranquility at Shaba to raise and study Penny, by which time George had retreated to Kora to continue with his lion rehabilitation work. His book *My pride and Joy* describes those years. Both Joy and George were to die violently, not by the felines to which they both devoted the end years of their lives, but at the hand of man.

The Adamsons drove and walked over great distances in northern Kenya. They approached the twenty-four-metre drop of Chanler's Falls along a rough riverside track, where Joy on her 1951 painting safari had found a fossilised spindle shell. The last half-mile was

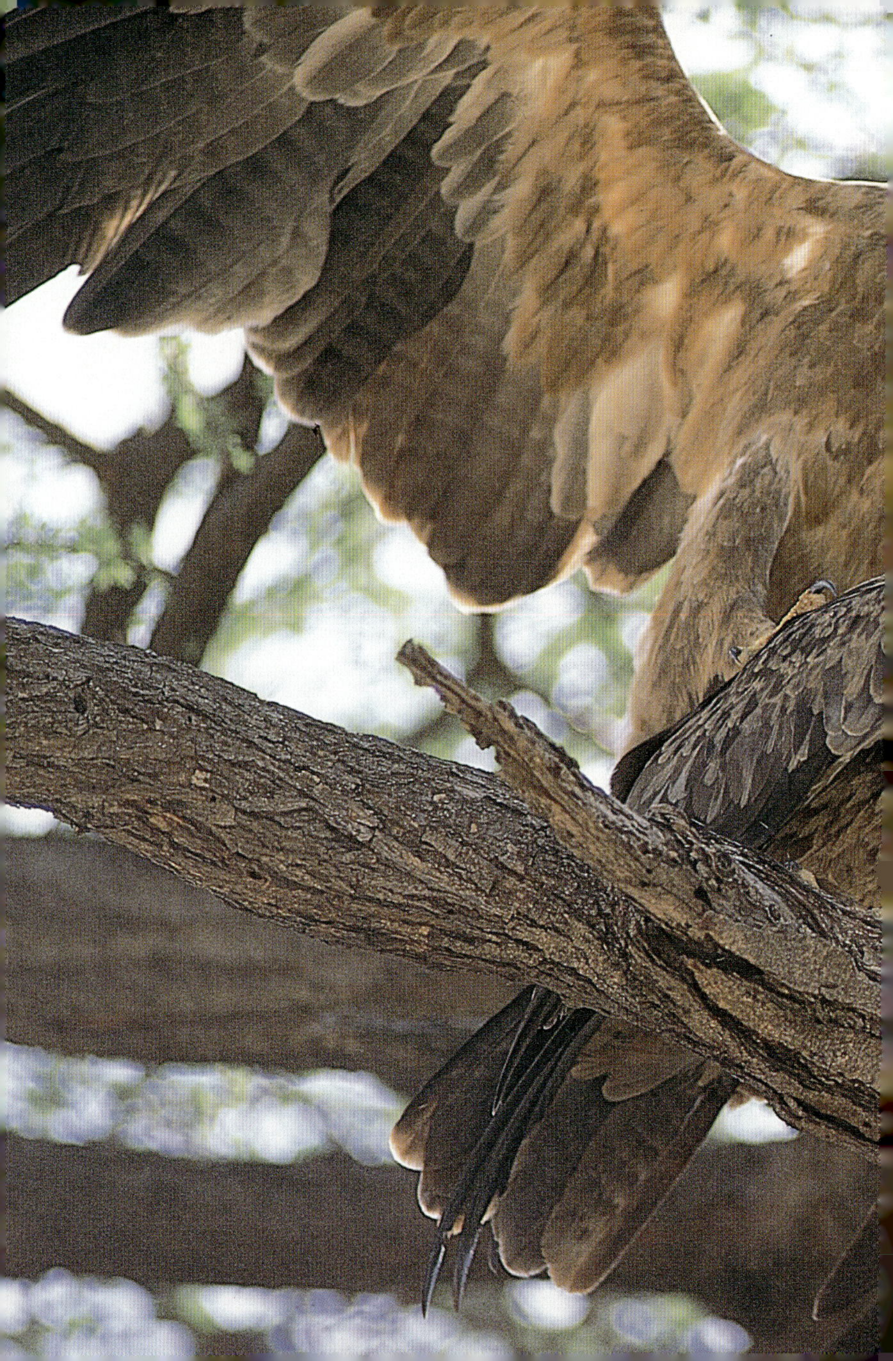

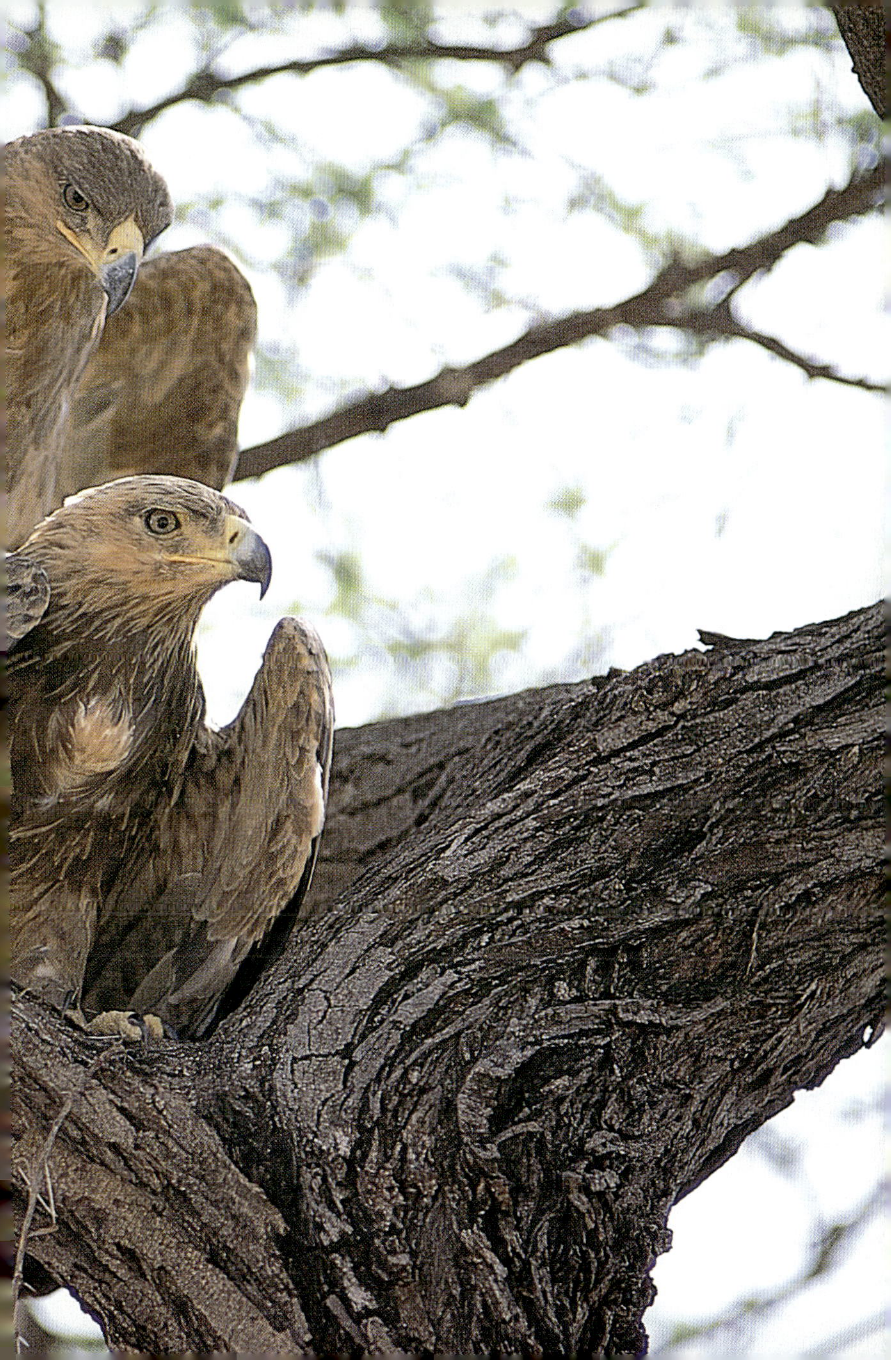

through a natural vault in the rock face, the foot of the vault almost level with the river's normal height, but impassable when the river is in flood which it can be quite suddenly.

There are two alternative ways from Shaba for today's travellers to the Chanler's Falls but in the 1990s it became necessary to check the outside-reserve security situation for both routes before starting off. Disturbed conditions in Somalia and severe famine throughout northern Kenya and Somalia seriously affected Kenya's north-east.

Given the necessary clearance, one route is to cross the reserve from west to east on the in-park road to the Gafarsa Gate and, conditional upon getting the security all-clear there, to continue on eastwards outside the reserve to where, below 970-metre Tumtu, the Losesia, a tributary of the Uaso Nyiro, joins the main river.

The other route is outside the reserve by the road to Merti from Archer's Post. Very rough in parts it should only be attempted with four-wheel drive. Eastwards from Archer's Post and north of the river it passes Bodich and 1,480-metre Kamanga, with Tumtu ahead. On this road, half–way between Chanler's Falls and Merti, old Kenya maps show 'Kittermaster's Camp', the one-time base on the Uaso Nyiro of Harold Baxter Kittermaster when, in 1908 as Assistant District Commissioner, he took up his posting under Geoffrey Archer.

At 6 '7″ tall — 'the biggest and heaviest man ever to row in the Oxford (University) boat' — he topped Archer by a full inch. An impressive sight must have been the two giants striding along the river's banks together.

The journey from Sarova Shaba to Chanler's Falls takes half a day at least, even with an early start. For the two-way trip, a full day from dawn to sunset needs to be set aside. Food and ample liquid refreshments should be carried for there is no place to stay beyond

Overleaf: A David and Goliath encounter in the bush between elephant and obstreperous baboon.

the park.

An easier, shorter drive is to the Sharinka Falls which, below 945-metre Malkagalan, can be reached on the in-park circuit, as depicted on the reserve map.

A survey map of the area showing roads, tracks and river crossings is absolutely essential for adventures outside the reserve, one of which — security conditions permitting — might include a visit to the Magado Crater which is reached along a little-used road south of Chanler's Falls.

A wide circle of cliffs, hidden by surrounding hills, guards the crater with its springs, salt lake and man-made wells, the only water for great distances around. Nomad herdsmen wait interminably to take turns to water their stock after taking the narrow, precipitous tracks down to the crater floor. Young girls drive donkeys carrying the precious water up and out, and salt, much prized for its flavour.

Not so very far from Shaba, Magado offers a sight literally 'out of this world' at this end of the twentieth century, and one upon which — even in recent years — few visitors to the district have looked. There, as the writer Errol Whittall once put it, is evidence in its simplest form of 'Man's ageless fight for survival in the desert places of the world.'

The crater lies approximately three-quarters of the way from the Uaso Nyiro at Chanler's Falls and the road from Isiolo to Garissa (the C 84).

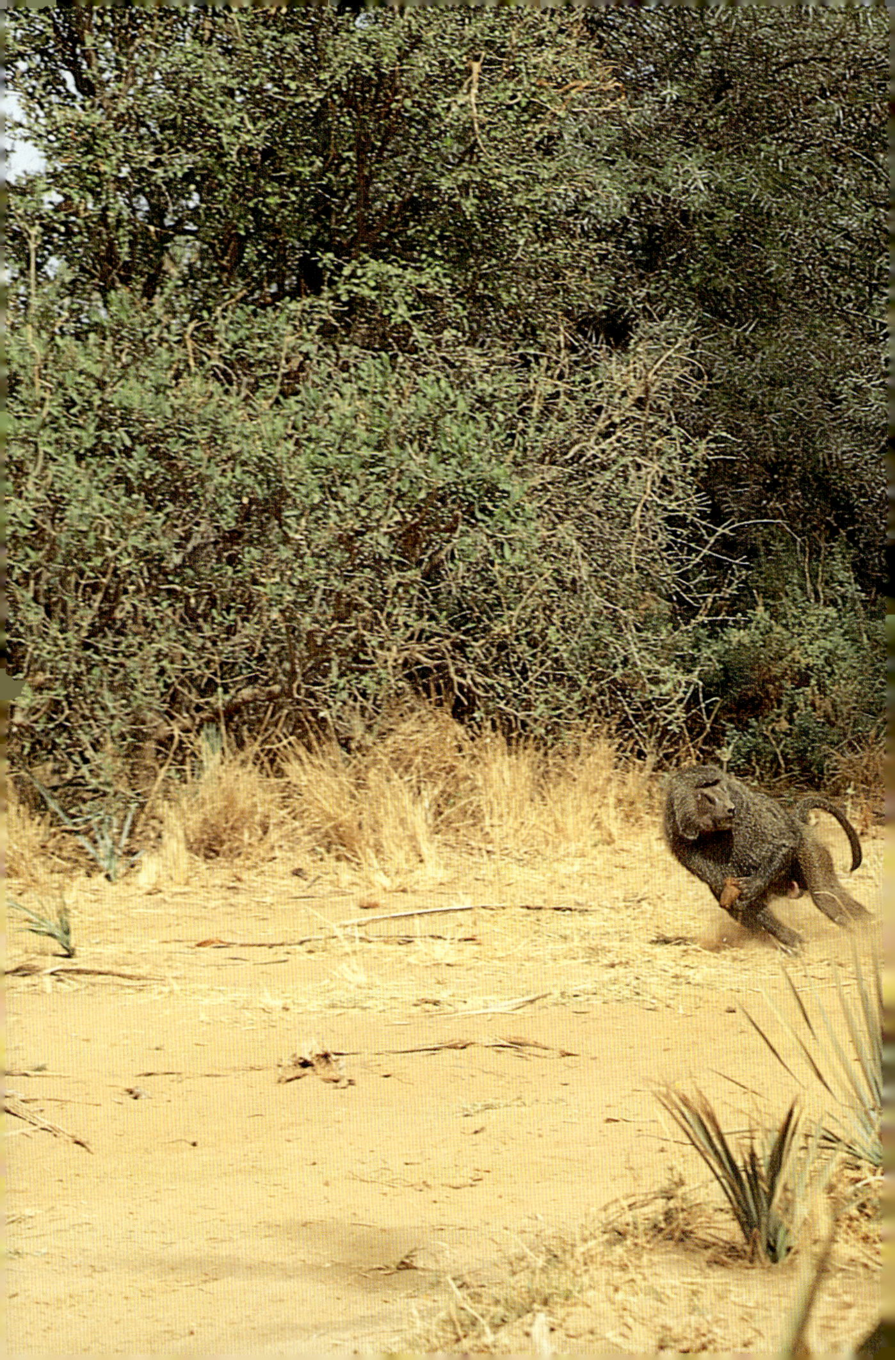

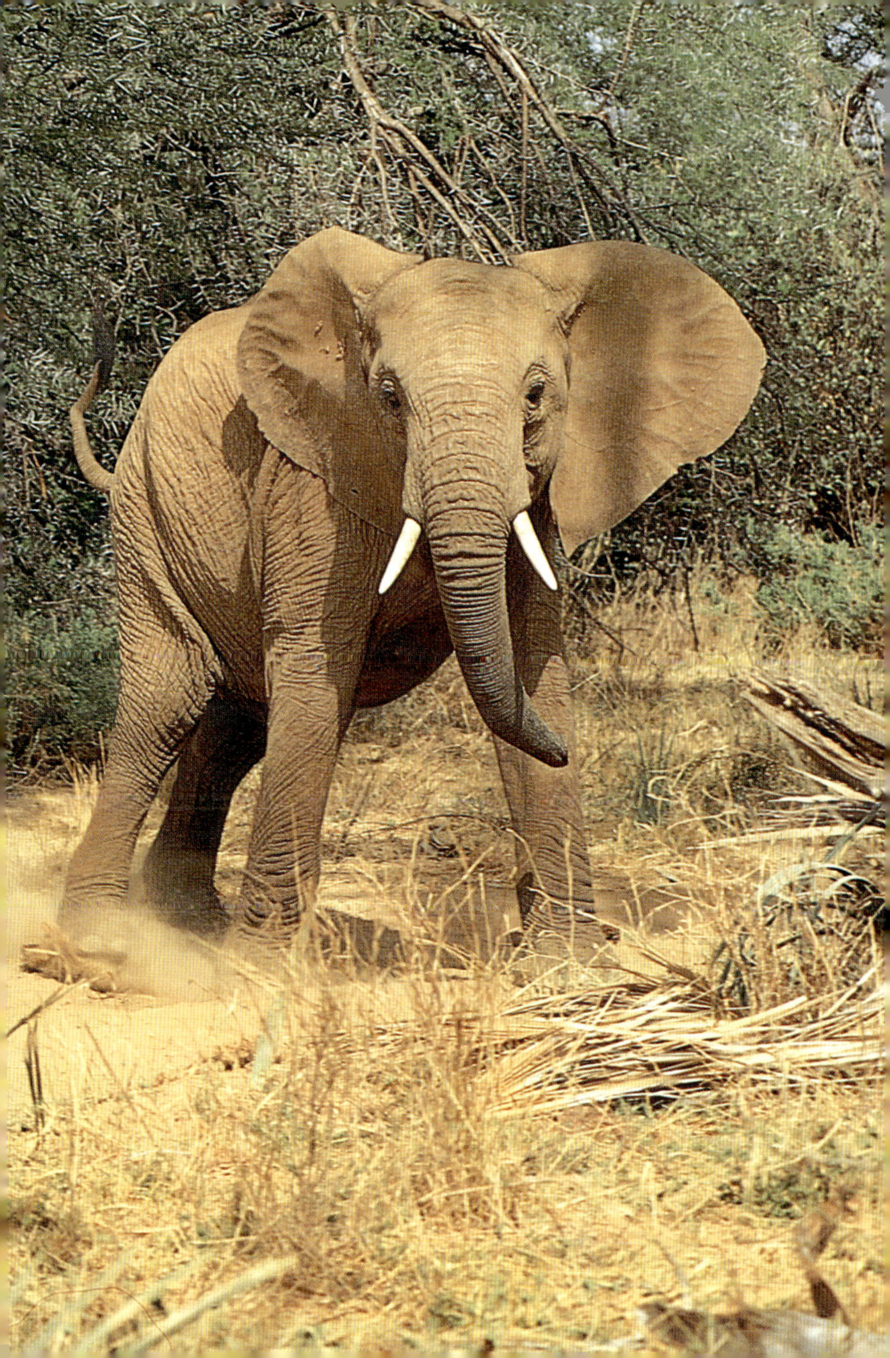

6. The Lion and the Unicorn

All the 'Big Five' — elephant, rhino, buffalo, lion and leopard — call these three reserves their home, and two of the most favoured subjects of fantasy and fable, the lion and the unicorn.

Shaba is quite one of the best places in Kenya for seeing large herds of Beisa oryx, which also inhabit the two other reserves. The Kilimanjaro, or fringe-eared oryx is not found in these parts.

Creature of myth and heraldry, was it the Beisa oryx (*Oryx beisa annectens*) with its magnificent long, rapier-like horns — to which many a lion has succumbed fatally — which was the origin of the legendary unicorn? Or even the 'Kilimanjaro' fringe-eared oryx (*Oryx beisa callotis*)? History is not clear.

Four hundred years before Christ, the Greek physician and historian Ctesias, believed that the unicorn might really have been 'the one-horned Indian white wild ass', but Plato's pupil Aristotle accepted that it could have been either the 'so-called Indian white wild ass', as he put it, or the oryx. There was further confusion when the idea was introduced that it might even have been the narwhal — the sea-unicorn — or the rhinoceros.

As India became better known, the 'white wild ass' theory was discounted when it was realised that no such horned creature existed there, and beliefs in the unicorn's origins zoomed in on Africa, apparently ignoring the fact that there are, or once were — before modern mechanised hunting virtually exterminated them — Arabian oryx (*Oryx leucoryx*) in the Middle East, much whiter in colour than their African cousins.

Another theory was that the one-horned oryx illusion was the result of someone seeing one which had lost a horn through fighting, or had only been glimpsed in profile so that its two horns appeared to be one.

Overleaf: Creatures of myth and heraldry — Beisa oryx at Shaba.

All kinds of unlikely but fascinating legends surrounded the unicorn in the Middle Ages, a creature with the head and body of a horse, the hind legs of an antelope, a lion's tail (or sometimes the tail of a horse) and a long, sharp, twisted horn.

As a panacea against poison, when poisoning was a not uncommon means of getting rid of one's rivals or enemies, drinking cups were decorated with pictures of them. 'Unicorns horns' (from where could they have come?) were still being used in France as late as the eighteenth century for testing dishes put before royalty. Yet another legend was that if a 'unicorn' dipped its horns into a pool whilst drinking, whatever the condition of the water, it became purified. This would, indeed, have proved useful in some of Africa's muddier watering places.

Famous in heraldry, the milk-white unicorn of Scotland, huge, fierce and strong, opposite a lion rampant, still features in the British Royal Coat of Arms, but both of these 'Queen's Beasts', in colour and design, are a far cry from nature's own work, not least the beautifully marked beige-coloured oryx of East Africa with its broad white eye-stripe and muzzle and elegantly gartered forelegs.

In heraldry, the unicorn was the 'baddie', a 'lunar' creature, representing the moon, the night, darkness and evil. The lion was a 'solar' emblem, representing the sun, the day, or all that is light or good. Each seems a somewhat curious conception compared with their natural counterparts.

The lion of Samburu, Shaba and Buffalo Springs favour places within reach of drinking water, but in nothing like their numbers of fifty years ago. Like the indigenous people of Samburuland living outside the reserves, they are not sleek and well-fed but — more resembling Shakespeare's Cassius — 'have a lean and hungry look'.

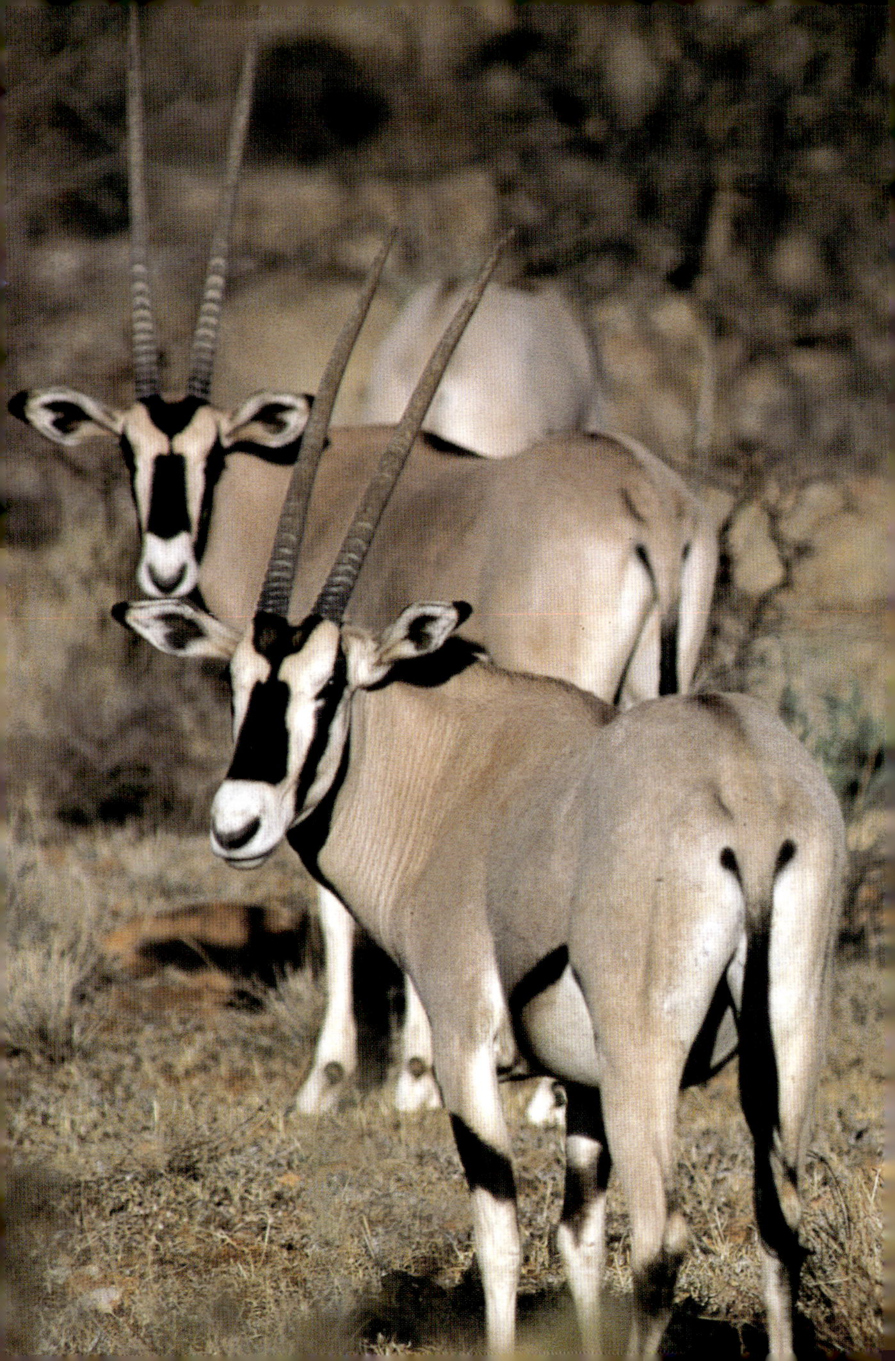

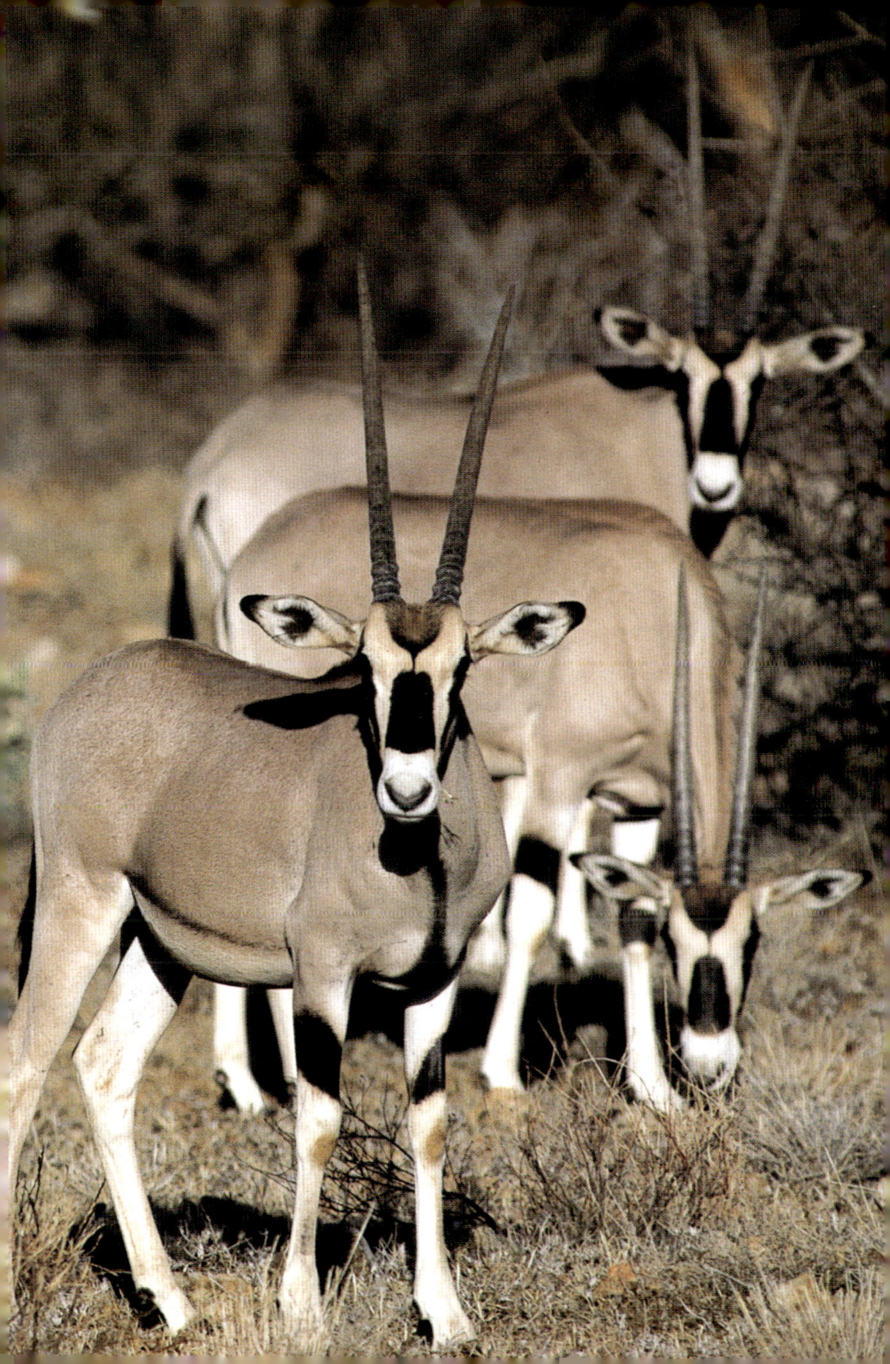

Their coats are rougher and sparser than those of the lions in the lusher parks. Because of the intense heat they will sometimes appear with their stringy coats caked with mud, when they have been able to find some cool, damp spot on which to lazily lie up during the hottest times of the day.

Cheetah somehow convey an impression of being the better fed, though it is doubtful if they are. Both sides of the river are reserved areas in the Samburu and Buffalo Springs reserves, and this is most often where they are found. Only the southern side of the river is reserved area in Shaba and the wildlife — ever wary of man — can sometimes be intimidated by nomads bringing their livestock down to drink on the opposite bank.

The zebra found in the north include the common zebra (sometimes called Burchell's and sometimes Grant's, *Equus burchelli granti*), which are also found in the south. Unlike further south, the three parks are the home of the Grevy zebra, the *Equus* (*dolichohippus*) *grevyi*, found in greater numbers there than elsewhere, though — now listed as Endangered Species by the International Union for the Conservation of Nature (IUCN) — not nearly as prolific as they used to be.

Heavier than the common zebra, they carry thick, high manes extending to their withers and are about a foot taller with larger rounded ears. Their stripes are narrow, and close together. From a distance, merging with the silver-grey scenery, they seem to be an almost all-over pale grey. France's nineteenth-century president, Jules Grevy, was responsible for their name, having been made a gift of one by the King of Shoa in 1881. Gerenuk, impala, eland and reticulated giraffe are also found in the north, and three species found in many other reserves and national parks — Thomson's and

Grant's gazelles and Kirk's dik-dik. Guenther's dik-dik, larger than the Kirk's, is a northern species, but is more likely to be found further north still at Marsabit.

Buffalo (*Syncerus caffer caffer*) inhabit the swamp areas — Buffalo Springs was not idly named — and waterbuck graze the plains bordering the river. Leopard, like cheetah, favour rocky outcrops and river fringes where the plains game are their prey.

In the trees across the river from Samburu Lodge, their arrival usually heralded by a cacophony of noisy protest from the baboon who habitually sleep there (will they never learn?), leopard are lured nightly by bait hung out for them when, for the benefit of viewers and patient photographers staying in the lodge, the trees are floodlit.

Opportunist vervet monkeys are prevalent wherever there are trees, particularly the *Ficus sycamorus* along the river banks where the monkeys, baboons and birds all enjoy its fruit. They also accumulate in the lodge grounds and around the camp sites — keep your eyes on that sugar bowl — optimistic of easy takings. Colonies of baboon and packs of hyena roam the three parks.

Among the smaller mammals most likely to be encountered, particularly in the Samburu reserve, are ground squirrels. These delightful and entertaining golden-brown small creatures are quite abundant around Samburu Lodge where they have no fear of people.

Genet cats around the lodges scamper freely through the open dining rooms and verandahs in the hope of finding some morsel or other, purposely or inadvertently dropped from the tables.

The hyrax around the lodges are also semi-tame, but hare, mongoose, wart hog, civet, serval, porcupine, klipspringer, ant bear and zorilla remain wild.

There are some massive leopard tortoises (*Geochelone pardalis*)

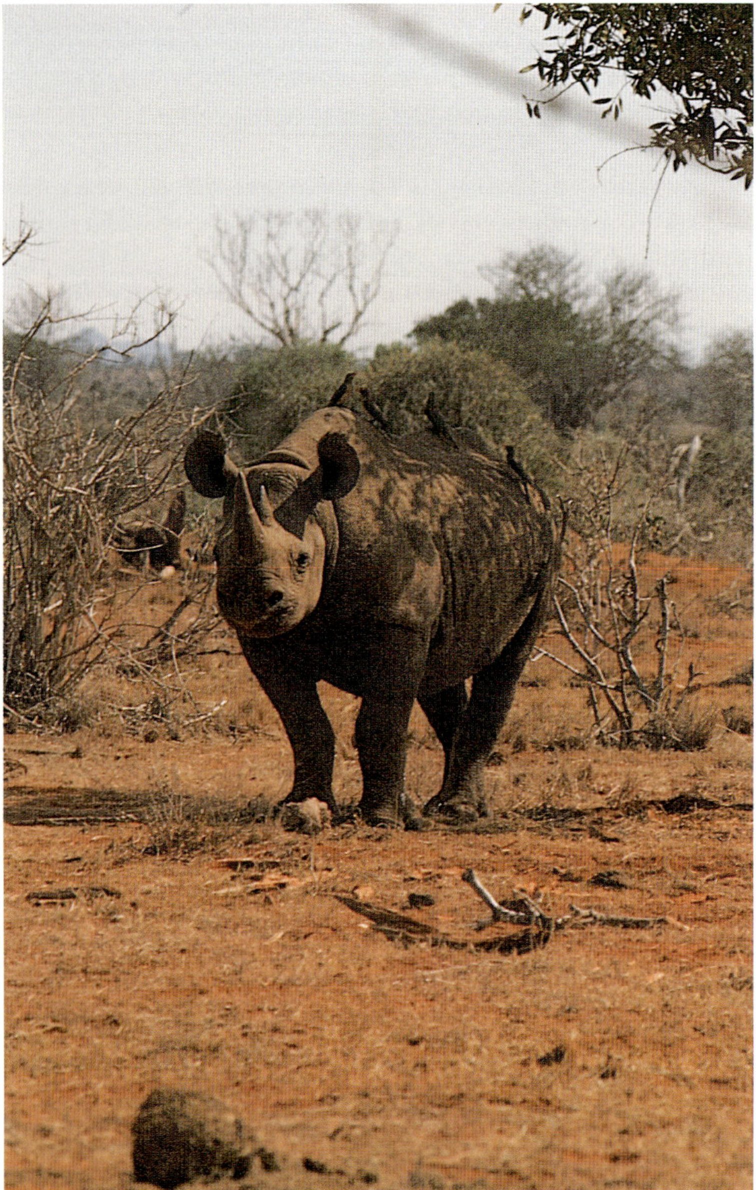

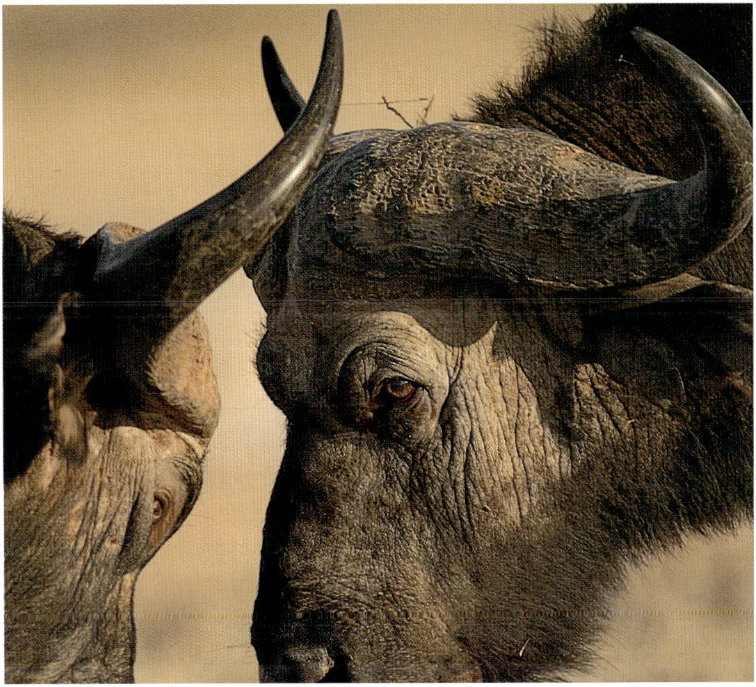

Above: African Buffalo (Syncerus caffer) *'the wild black cattle of Africa'.*

Right: Guenther's dik-dik (Rhychotragus guentheri) *the delicate small antelopes common to Kenya's north.*

Opposite: The Black (hook-lipped) rhino (Diceros bicornis) *has rounded, almost hairless ears. The horns of the females are shorter than the males.*

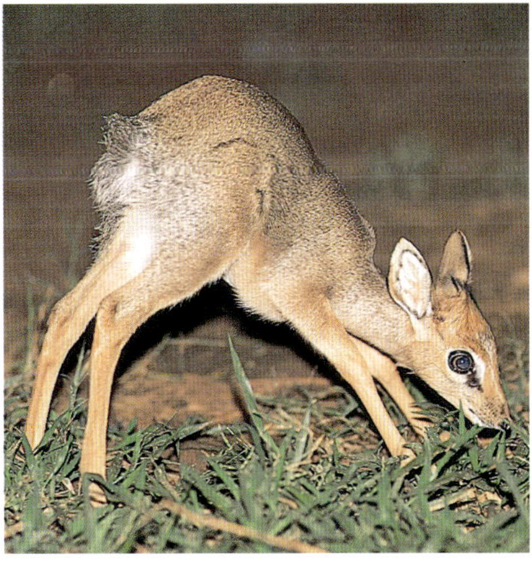

rearing their families on the river banks below Samburu Lodge which, because of their size, must have been alive in Neumann's time. It is not unusual for them to live a hundred years or more and, like ageing members of the judiciary, give the impression of looking out on their surroundings with world-weary saurian eyes.

Brilliantly-coloured agama lizards (*Agama lionotus*) with their red or orange-coloured heads, cerulean backs and darker blue bodies are worthy of any photographer's attention, sunning themselves wherever there are rocks and stones. If alarmed or sensing danger, however, like chameleons they will disguise themselves by changing their wonderful colours to match their immediate surroundings.

Other small species include otters, bats and mole rats.

The river and its banks are home to some immense Nile crocodile (Mamba in Kiswahili), river crocodiles which are generally people-eaters as well as being partial to lesser and larger prey. Cheeky ratels (honey badgers), which farmers and poultrymen in Kenya hate because they generally cause havoc in the farm outhouses by stealing eggs and are ruthless and daring killers of chickens and ducks, all too often in the wild themselves become the victims of the crocodiles when venturing too close to their gaping jaws. Their right to survive, whatever the farmers may say, is championed by C T Astley Maberly in his *Animals of East Africa*. 'The ratel (*Mellivora capensis sagulata*, in Kiswahili, Nyegere) is one of the most admirable little beasts in Africa. Normally inoffensive and peacefully inclined, it will attack at once if interfered with — no matter what the odds. Having a singularly tough and elastic skin it will stand the severest mauling from several dogs without apparent harm, but will usually inflict such punishment on its adversaries that it frequently wins the day. Like a European badger, once it gets a tooth-hold, the ratel hangs on till the bitter end and nothing, short of death, will usually dislodge it. It is a famed killer of snakes.'

In the water, it is the harmless terrapin whose lives are most constantly at risk. A popular crocodile pastime is snapping at them nastily. Or perhaps crocodile collectively just respond to an instinct which demands that if anything moves — eat it.

With patience, determination and a good safari guide, black rhino, *Diceros bicornis bicornis* (Kifaru, sometimes just Faru, in Kiswahili) may still be seen in each of the three parks but, like the lion, the 'unicorn' and the elephant, alas, in nothing like the numbers that they used to be.

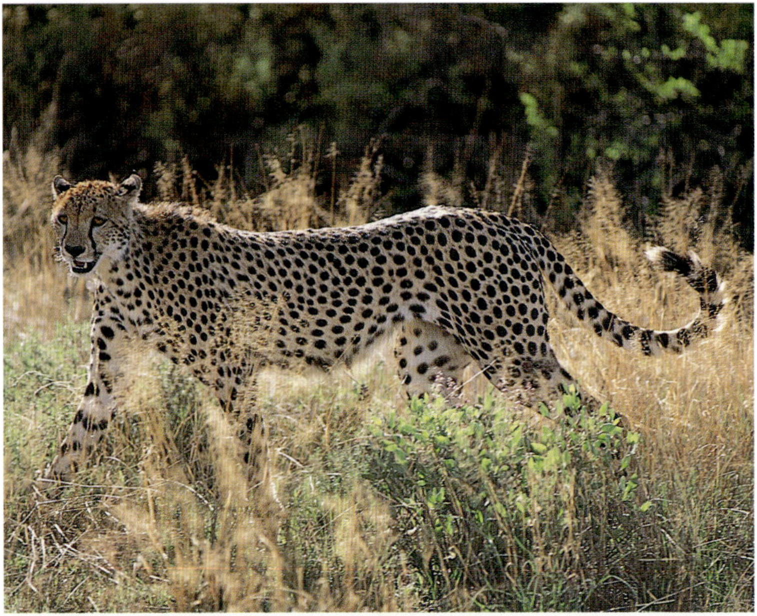

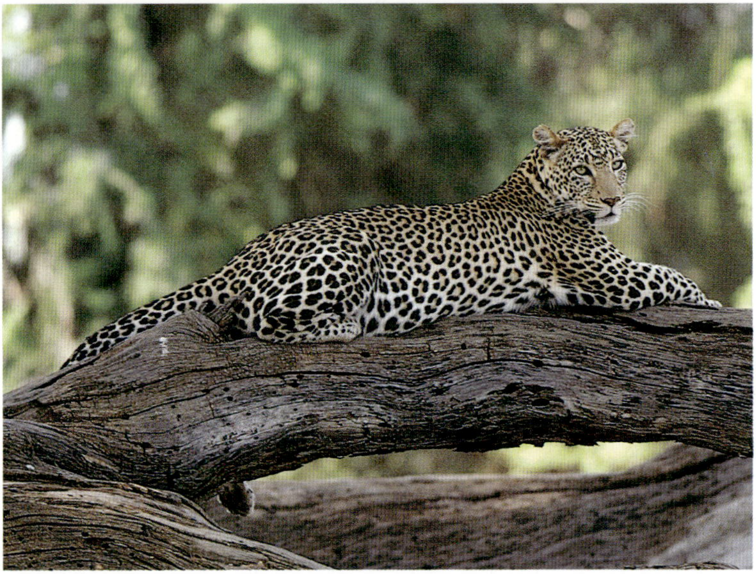

*Opposite top: The spots on the cheetah (*Acinonyx jabatus*) are round, as compared with the rosettes of the leopard (*Panthera pardus*).*
Opposite bottom: Lying out on a branch, in dappled sunlight and shade, a leopard's camouflage is virtually complete.
*Below: The common genet (*Genetta genetta*) is frequently seen around Samburu Lodge.*

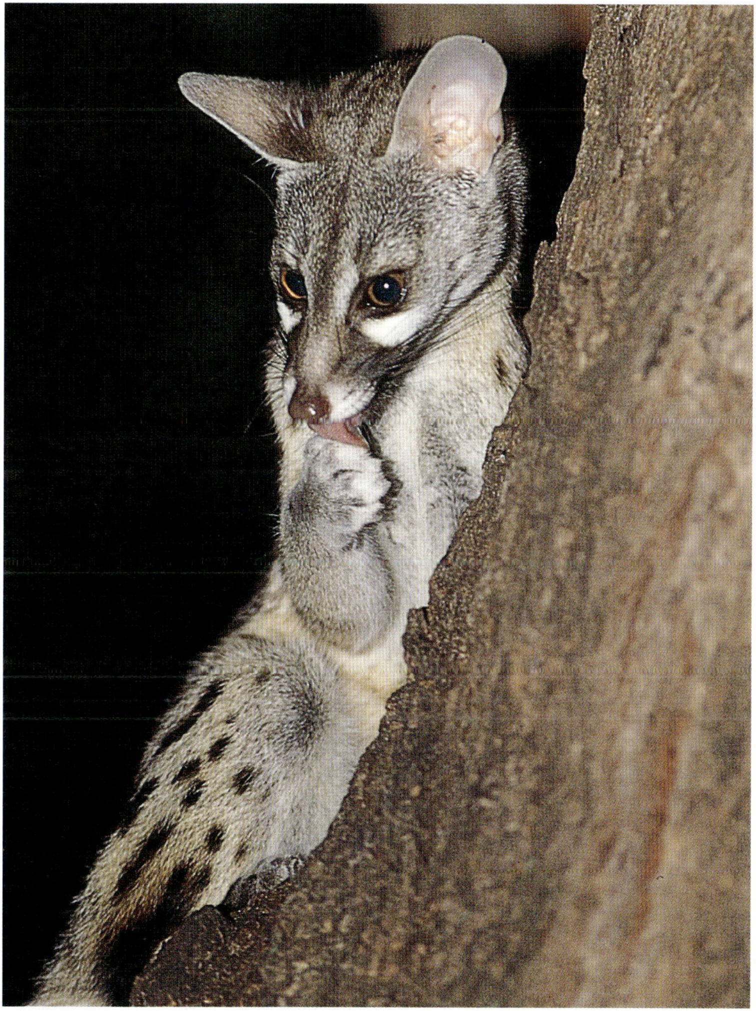

7. The Birds and the Bees

Much of the beauty of the Samburu, Shaba and Buffalo Springs reserves is contributed by the birdlife for, although some of the northern avifauna — particularly the females, rarely so conspicuous as the males — tend toward fawns and browns which give them their natural camouflage, there are sufficient bright and beautiful birds to glorify their surroundings in a way which few other features of the landscape can do. They merit an exploration of the three-park complex in their own right.

In common with all the other creatures of the wild, they are beset by predators, not all of which by any means are bigger, stronger birds. Some display a sense of humour and fun which is of great human appeal. Examples might be the honey guide, whose performances could be regarded as award-winning, and those sex maniacs the hammerkops whose noisy proclamations that they are 'at it again' (and again, and again, and again) invite new interpretations of 'mating for life'.

The seemingly demented greyish-brown bird persistently jumping up and down in front of you, in a manner little short of frenzied, chattering noisily to attract your 'undivided', will be the greater or black-throated honey guide, telling and showing you — repeatedly — that if only you will follow it to a nearby tree, there will be honey there. It has no interest in the honey. For all it cares, you are very welcome to the lot. The attractions are those exquisite delicacies of wax, larvae and grubs which the smashed honeycombs will provide. When the honey guide enlists the help of the honey badger (ratel) in its search for hives, as the bird sometimes does, a share will be wanted of the delectables.

Beyond the reserved areas — and not unknown in them — this modestly coloured bird with pink beak and greyish-white underparts, will fearlessly lead you — as the Latin name *Indicator indicator* suggests — to man-made hives hung in trees near human habitation. These might be hollowed-out sections of tree-trunk suspended from the branches of spreading acacias, or any other receptacle likely to make a 'Des. Res.' for African wild bees — much shorter tempered than their European cousins and prone to turning nasty at the slightest provocation or even without it.

In twitters and whistles the honey-seeking Wandorobo will 'talk' to the honey guide, encouraging it to lead them to the wild honey which is their only form of sugar. Whether Kilalisho, the controversial Captain Richard Meinertzhagen's lance-corporal, was led to what he found in a hollow tree beside the Uaso Nyiro River by a honey guide is not said in Meinertzhagen's *Kenya Diary 1902-1906*, only that the unfortunate captain found it to be a powerful emetic which incapacitated him for the rest of the day.

Popular as they are with humans, and their rather endearing guiding habits apart, the honey guide is not quite so kindly disposed towards other birds. Parasitic, they lay their eggs in the nests of other species, especially those of woodpecker, bee-eater and barbet, all of which inhabit these northern reserves.

The greater honey guide, about twenty centimetres in length, is found in arid thornbush and acacia country and in woodlands of all kinds. The grey-billed scaly-throated honey guide (*Indicator variegatus*), slightly smaller at nineteen centimetres, will most likely be found where trees flank the river.

The lesser honey guide (*Indicator minor*), its upperparts a dull olive and its underparts pale greyish-white, is smaller at around fourteen centimetres. Smaller still, Wahlberg's honey guide (P*rodotiscus regulus*), is around eleven centimetres and might just be seen in a

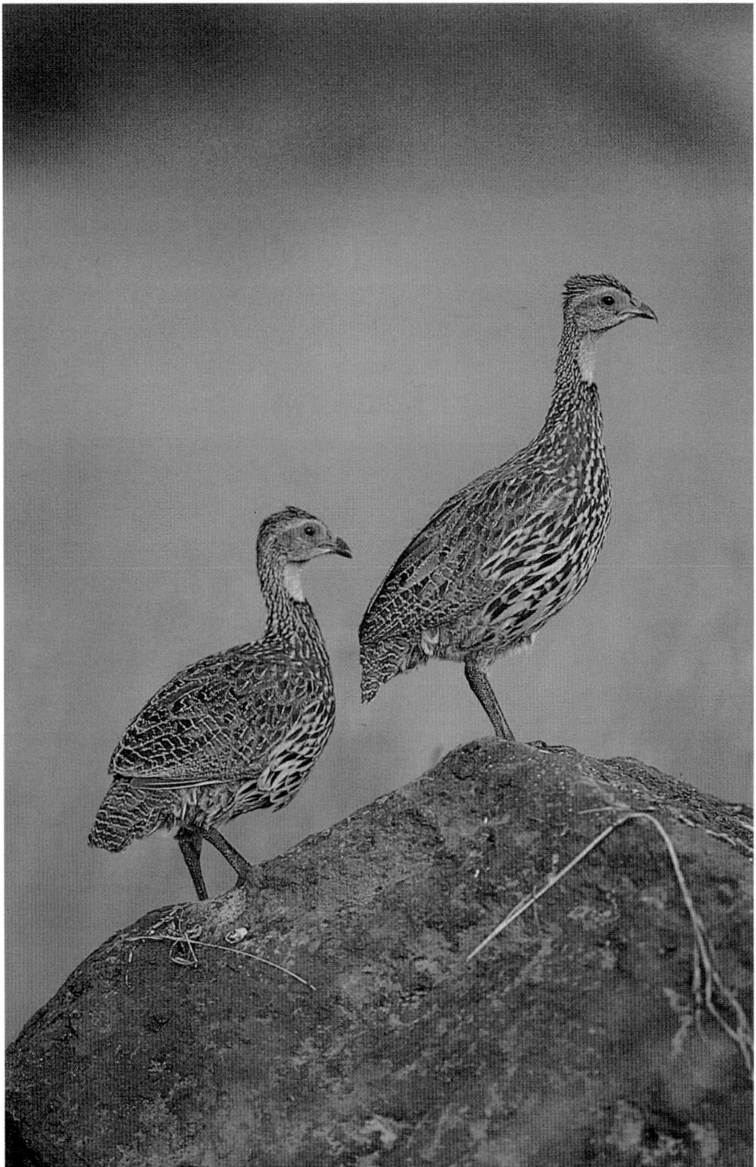

*Opposite: Yellow-necked spurfowl (*Pternistis leucoscepus*) the commonest of Kenya's francolins.*

*Below: Lilac-breasted roller (*Coracias caudata*). The lilac in the northern species is confined to the foreneck and throat.*

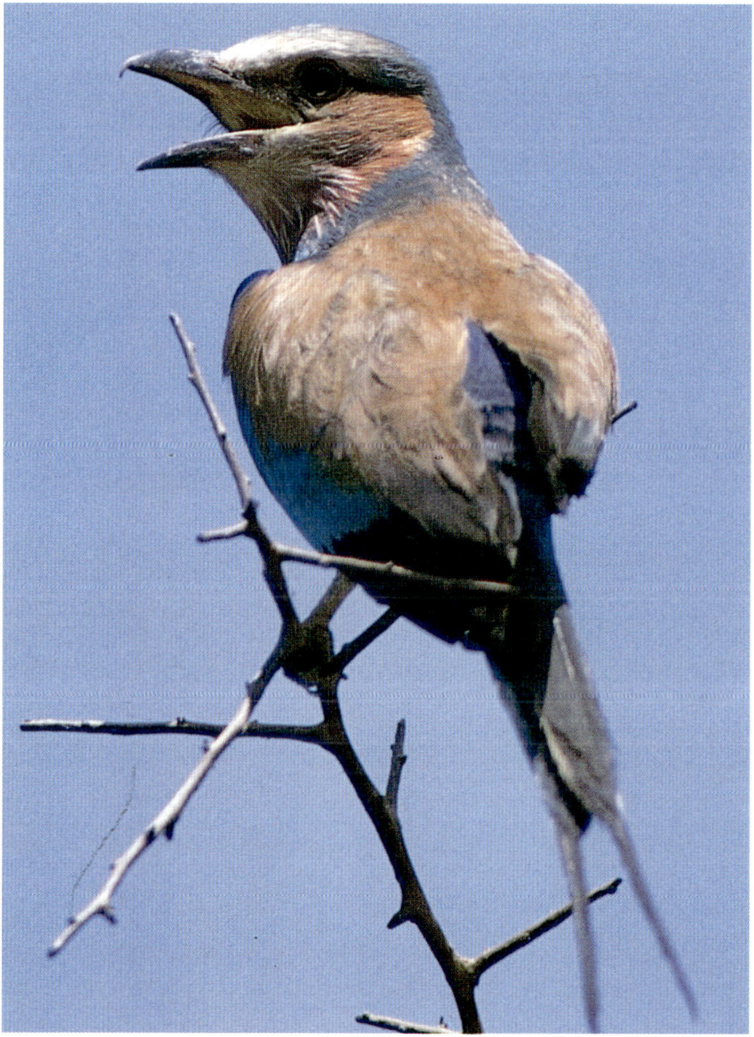

yellow-barked acacia along the river bank where it sits almost motionless.

The least likely honey guide to be found in this region is the Wahlberg's olive-plumaged look-alike, Cassin's honey guide (*Prodotiscus insignis*), which prefers East and Central Africa's more forested, and therefore usually colder, regions.

It is a case of 'eat or be eaten' for most of the creatures of these scorching wildlands where, as more than one naturalist has had cause to complain, 'everything either burns or bites'. Bees are the preferred diet of the bee-eater. Those most likely to be seen there are the resident or partially migrant little bee-eater (*Melittophagus pusillus*), small, green, with yellow throat, blue-black neck-patch and black eye-streak, and, with luck, the glorious and unmistakable carmine bee-eater (*Merops nubicus*) which, as a resident and partial migrant, favours dry bush country.

How do birds survive in lands where there is no ground water? Much of the birdlife of these parts is around the rivers and the *luggas* — the seasonal rivers which dry up for long periods of the year — or within flying distance of them. Beyond the rivers and springs, however, lie the vast, truly barren desert areas.

It is there that the Samburu, Rendille and Boran people, for both domestic consumption and for their livestock, dig wells in the dried-up watercourses. As the drought intensifies, the digging goes deeper and deeper to reach the water table. A human ladder of as many as five, six or even seven men is sometimes needed to hand the water from one to the other to the surface, where it is tipped into the cattle troughs constructed around the hole. Few, if any birds, however desperate, are known to fly down underground, but the gregarious blue-eared glossy starling (*Lamprocolius chalybaeus*) of Samburuland, not even terrorised, as might be expected, by the regular chanting and continuous activity of the chain of bucket-lifters, fly deep down into the wells.

On the surface, the girls and women of the family or clan to which the well belongs, gather their water from the troughs. The cattle are watered every other day, but the sheep and goats may have to wait up to three days, usually driven to the wells from distant grazing grounds by the younger children. The long-suffering camels may probably only be taken to slake their thirsts at the troughs every ten days or more, but they are sturdy creatures and, like the cows and the goats, are the providers of milk.

Many other types of starling are found throughout the three parks and beyond. It is one of the best places for seeing small groups of golden-breasted starling (*Cosmopsarus regius*), also known as the regal starling, widely regarded as quite one of the most beautiful birds of Africa. A true inhabitant of Samburu and other dry, thornbush country, with its brilliant green-blue upperparts and golden belly it is one of the most easily identified, but not easy to get near to.

Superb starling (*Spreo superbus*) are common, and confident enough around the lodges, to fly onto the breakfast table, plump, short-tailed, metallic blue and green, blackish head, chestnut belly and narrow white band across the breast.

Wattled starling (*Creatophora cinerea*), intent upon reducing the hot land's insect life — almost any flying insect will do but they are very partial to locusts, which arc usually around after the rains — will be found in the acacia woodlands as well as in the thornbush country, pale grey birds with whitish rump and black wings and tail.

In the breeding season the male wattled starling falls fashion's

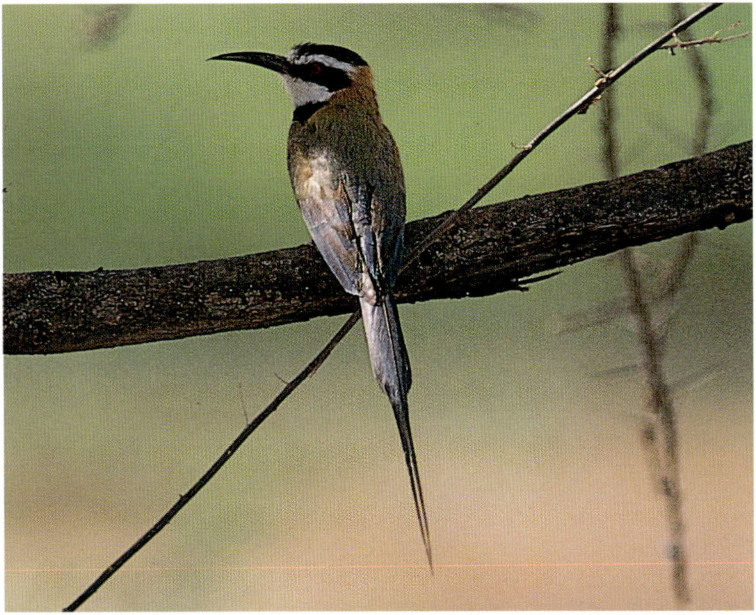

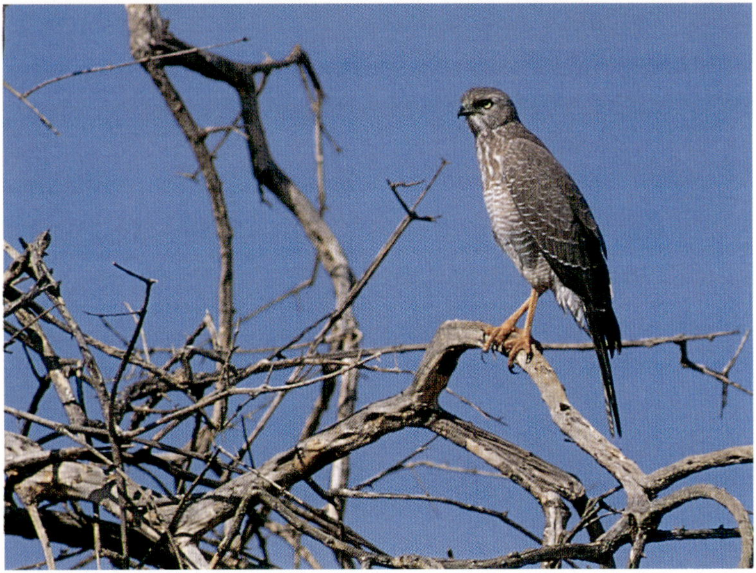

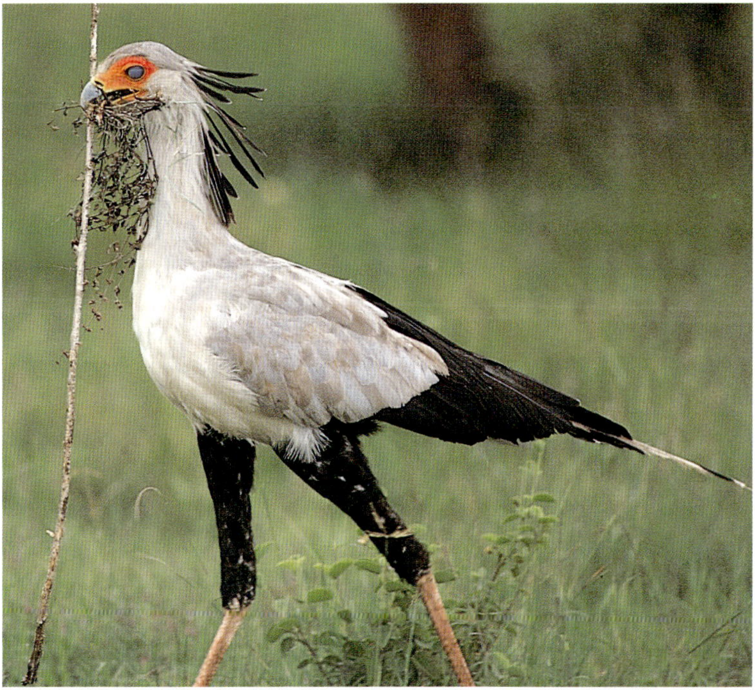

Above: Secretary bird (Sagittarius serpentarius), *conspicuous by its long crest feathers and solemn dignity.*

Right. Cheeky Superb starlings (Spreo superbus) *are confident invaders of the open-air breakfast table.*

Opposite top: White-throated bee-eater (Aerops albicollis) *mainly a passage migrant.*

Opposite bottom: The pale chanting goshawk (Melierax poliopterus) *is well known in the semi-desert country.*

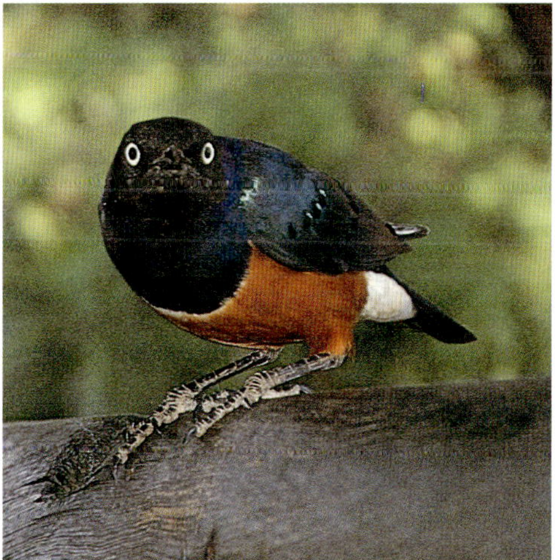

victim with the 'skinhead look'. Loosing his feathers, his head is then a waspish yellow and black. The bird's three wattles are responsible for its name, on forehead, crown and throat.

Weavers, a gregarious species generally, are there in force: the white-browed sparrow weaver (*Plocepasser mahali*); the masked weaver (*Ploceus intermedius*), mainly yellow but with a streaked, olive-green mantle; the white-headed buffalo weaver (*Dinemellia dinemelli*), brown and white with orange-red rump and under tail coverts, usually seen in small flocks; the grey-headed social weaver (*Pseudonigrita arnaudi*), greyish-brown with a pale grey cap; that very handsome fellow the chestnut weaver (*Ploceus rubiginosus*), bright chestnut with black head and throat; the vitelline masked weaver (*Ploceus vitellinus*), similar to the masked weaver but with mainly chestnut crown and narrow black frontal band. The 'Golden Ones' are the golden-backed weaver (*Ploceus jacksoni*), the golden palm weaver (*Ploceus bojeri*) and Holub's golden weaver (*Xanthophilus xanthops*), most likely to be found in chattering numbers wherever there are swamps and marshes.

Kingfisher, near the water, will be the grey-headed (*Halcyon leucocephala*) with its black and cobalt upperparts, blue wing feathers, rump and tail; the enchanting, jewel-coloured malachite (*Corythornis cristata*); the pygmy (*Ispidina picta*) — the tiniest kingfisher — ultramarine upperparts, orange-rufous with lilac wash on the back of neck, orange-rufous underparts and red bill; the more clerical-looking black and white pied kingfisher (*Ceryle rudis*) and the giant (*Megaceryle maxima*), with crested head and slatey-grey upperparts finely spotted with white.

Hammerkop (*Scopus umbretta*) will be found wherever water provides them with a diet of frogs to sustain them in their remarkable mating activities (some twenty times in the morning and again in the late afternoon) to which these large, crested, donkey-brown pairs of look-alike males and females immodestly shriek for attention with their repeated 'Yeh! Yeh! Yeh! Yeh! Yeh! Yeh! Oh yeah! Oh yeah! Oh YEAH!'

Cormorants favouring the sandbanks, egrets, darters, sacred and hadada ibis, herons, storks and wagtails are all seen along or near the river.

The three reserves, especially in the riverine trees near the lodges, are excellent places for seeing hornbill and their curious nesting habits, shared by all those of the Tockus genus: von der Decken's (*Tockus deckeni*), white-breasted with black wings, the bill red but ending white; the red-billed (*Tockus erythrorhynchus*) and the yellow-billed (*Tockus flavirostris*).

With home-making in mind, the male and female hornbill choose a hole in a tree which they then start to plaster over with mud. When the female enters their almost completed work she seals herself in with her own droppings and in this retreat, safe from predators, lays her eggs (two, three or four of them) and sits on them, all the while fed by the male from the outside through a narrow slit. She moults during this period, becoming flightless, but after six or seven weeks when the young have been hatched and are part grown, she breaks open the nest entrance and emerges, leaving the young inside. By this time she has grown new feathers and seems none the worse for her incarceration. She will help the male to feed their brood, who have sealed themselves in again. They will not be ready to break out themselves until their feathers have grown.

Turaco seen in the parks are the Ross's (*Musophaga rossae*), violet-black with crimson flight feathers, crest and orange-yellow face and

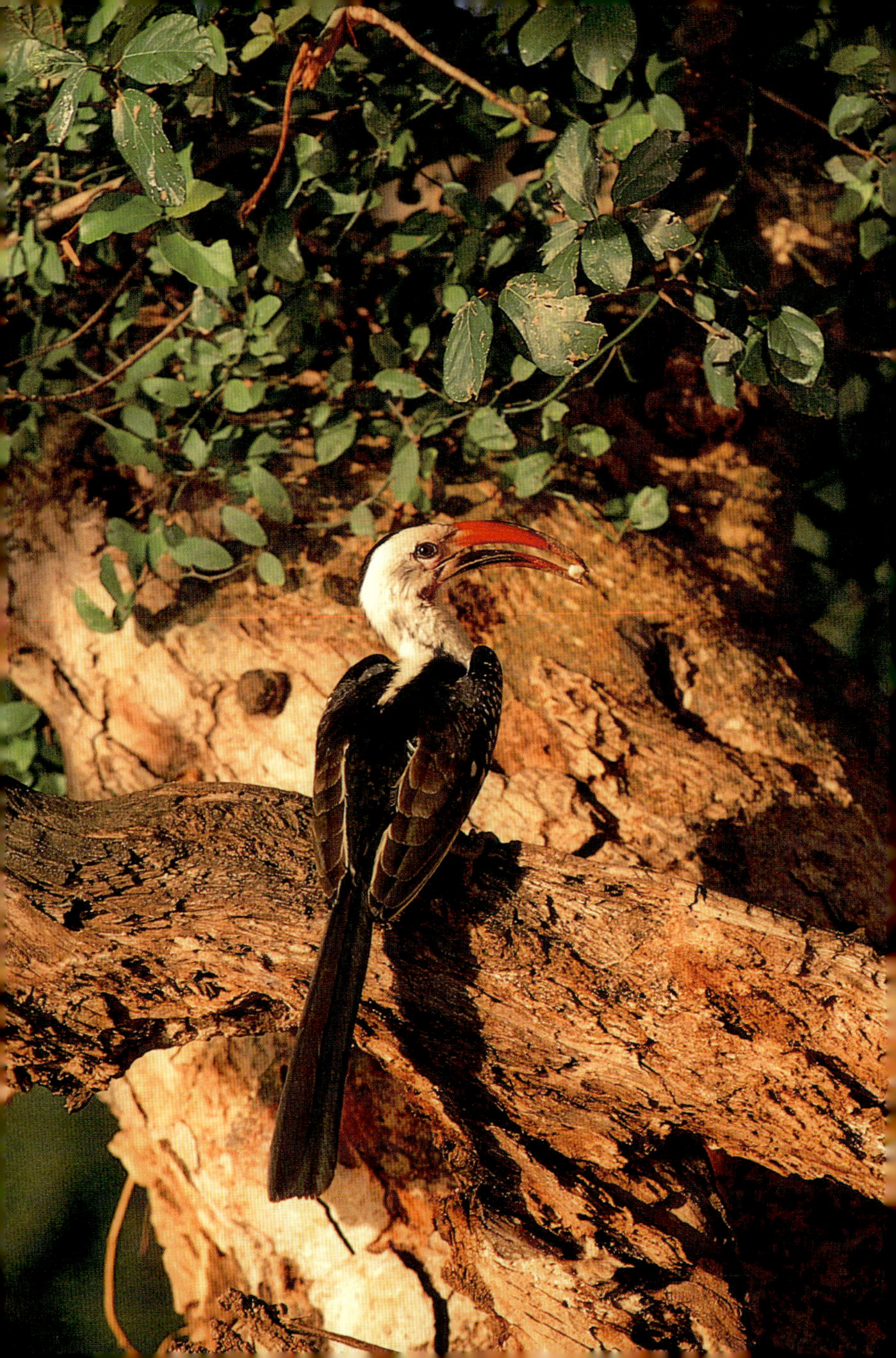

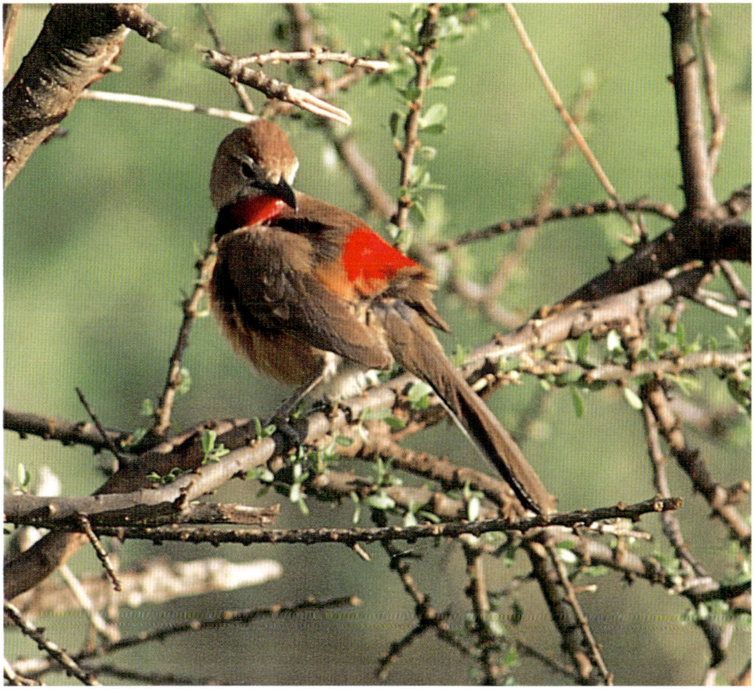

Above: Rosy-patched shrike (Rhodophoneus cruentus) *are seen frequently at Shaba.*

Right: The Carmine bee-eater (Merops nubicus) *is one of the most eye-catching birds of the north — greenish and cobalt-blue head and spectacular carmine upper and underparts.*

Opposite: The Red-billed hornbill (Tockus erythrorhynchus) *is common to all three reserves, particularly by the river.*

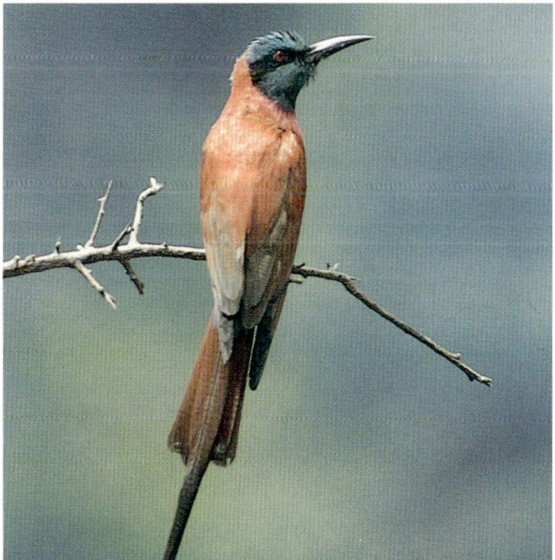

bill which clearly distinguish it from the Hartlaub's (*Tauraco hartlaubi*) with its violet-blue plumage, crimson flight feathers and green belly. Early in the year is the best time to see the Hartlaub's which fly in from miles around to gorge on the fruit of the *Ficus sycamorus* along the river banks.

Woodpecker — usually near the trees — will be the colourful cardinal (*Dendropicos fuscescens*), the crown and nape a beautiful scarlet in the male but not in the female; the Nubian (*Campethera nubica*), the crown and nape also scarlet in the male but black in the female, upperparts olive-grey spotted and yellowish-banded; the dusky bearded (*Thripias namaquus*), nape again red in the male but black in the female; and the grey (*Mesopicos goertae*). Not quite as dull as its name suggests, the male bird is certainly grey, but has a red crown and rump and sometimes a red streak down the centre of the belly. The back is golden-green.

Barbet, related to the woodpeckers, are local residents in Eastern Africa from Somalia down through Kenya to north-east Tanzania and those most likely to be seen in these parts are the red and yellow barbet (*Trachyphonus erythrocephalus*). Nesting in any holes they find, in river banks or in termite holes, they are usually seen in pairs, white-spotted on their strikingly yellow and red upperparts.

It was one of Kenya's most dedicated ornithologists, Leslie Brown — who knew his birds well — who referred to their 'astonishing cackling duets' as 'some of the most unlikely birdsounds of all.'

D'Arnaud's barbet (*Trachyphonus darnaudii*) with brownish, white-spotted body, black crown spotted with yellow and sides of face yellow spotted with black, also call in chorus. This pantomime requires two or more to face each other in order to be able to ceaselessly repeat their loud, four-note (and seemingly endless) aria.

Shrike are also duettists and so inevitably come in pairs. The repeated call of the slate-coloured bou bou shrike (*Laniarius funebris*) is a three or four bell-like whistle from one of them and a rusty croak from the other. The rosy-patched shrike (*Rhodophoneus cruentus*) — seen often near Sarova Shaba Lodge — is the most glamorous of the shrike family, pale pinkish-brown with rosy red rump and red on the breast and throat. The red rump is particularly striking in flight, giving a flash of colour across the arid distances.

Another noisy fellow is the white-bellied go-away bird (*Corythaixoides leucogaster*). Common to all three parks it shouts out its greeting — if a persistent 'Go Away' can be regarded as such — a grey, white and black dry-country species.

Doves seen — many of which seem to manage to keep up a constant coo-ing by day and by night — will be the Namaqua (*Oena capensis*), the subtly-shaded pink-breasted (*Streptopelia lugens*) and many other varieties common throughout Eastern Africa.

The Cuculidae — the cuckoo — will be the black and white (*Clamator jacobinus*); the red-chested (*Cuculus solitarius*), with its somewhat irritating insistance that "Rain will **come**, rain will **come**"; its allied species the black (*Cuculus cafer*) which is almost its black counterpart and found mostly along banks of the river; the greater spotted (*Clemator glandarius*) another allied species of the red-chested; Klaas' (*Chrysococcyx klaas*) — small, bright green with white underparts; and Didric's (*Chrysococcyx caprius*) also a metallic green.

The black-tipped crests of the African hoopoe (*Upupa africana*) are their distinguishing characteristic, almost like tiny helmets. These very attractive birds are most likely to be seen when feeding on the ground, but in flight are slow and undulating. Their plumage is a striking pinkish-rufous, white and black.

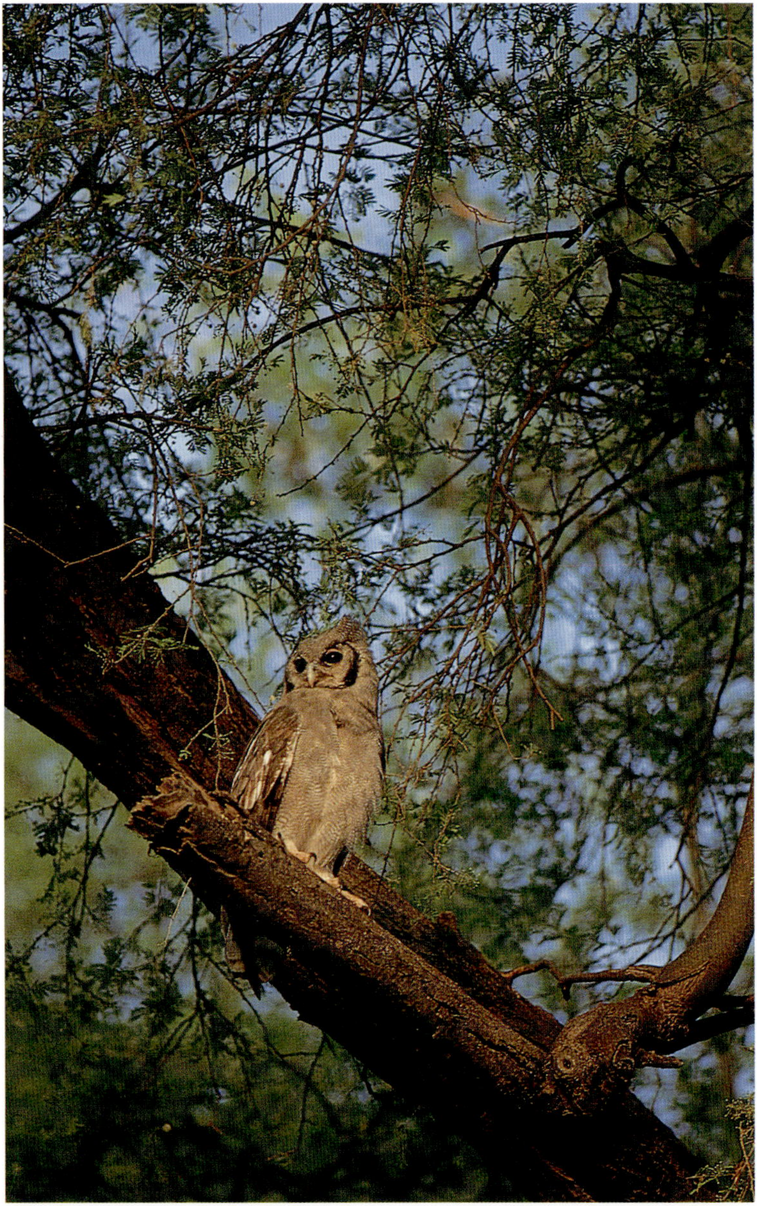

*Opposite: Best found in riverine trees, the black band each side of its face differentiates the Verreaux's eagle owl (*Bubo lacteus*) from Kenya's other nine owls and owlets.*

Below: The male Golden weaver builds a nest for his love which she may, or may not, accept.

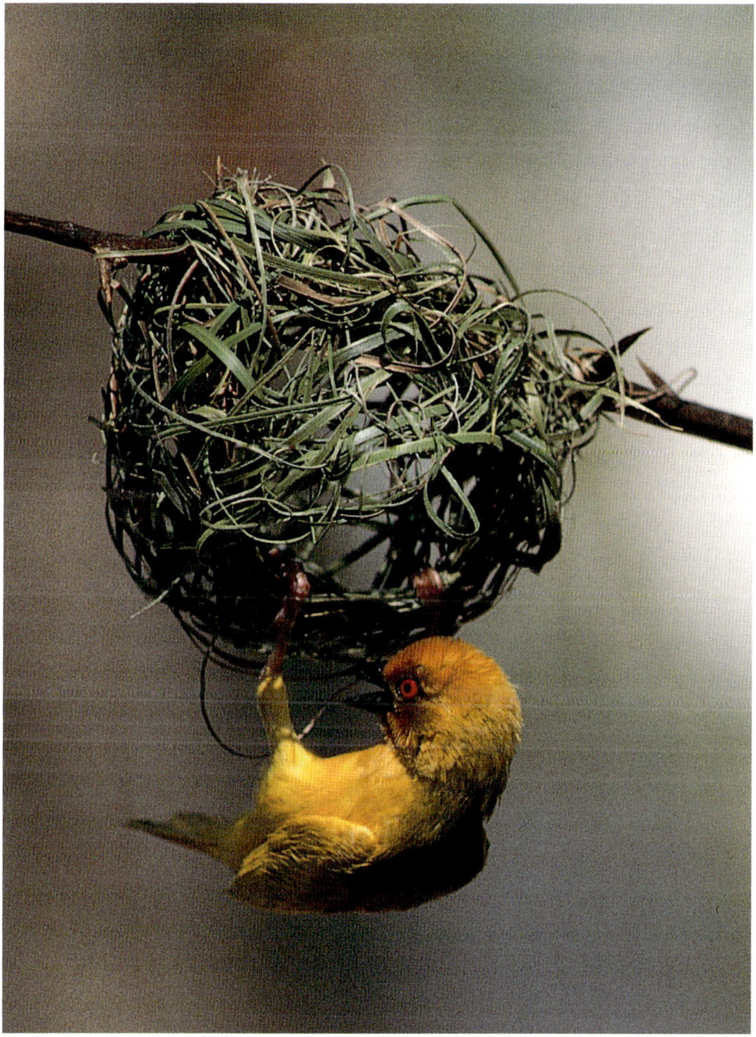

The lilac-breasted roller (*Coracias caudata*) is another glamorous beauty, a largish and comfortable-looking bird up to forty-one centimetres long from tip of bill to end of tail streamers. The lilac of their throats and breasts (males and females are alike) is offset by their tawny-brown upperparts, ultramarine blue rump and wing coverts.

Swift, swallow and martin, some resident, some partial migrants southwards from Ethiopia, are frequently seen near the water and around the lodges, making their homes under the eves and overhangs.

Sunbird, beautiful wherever they are found in Kenya and particularly in the barren north, are best seen around the riverine lodges in the Samburu reserve because of the flowers and garden cultivation. Nectar from the flowers must be a happy change for them — dessert as it were — after the insects which form their other major source of sustenance. They will be the variable (*Cinnyris venustus*); the mariqua (*Cinnyris mariquensis*) and the Somali scarlet-chested, more commonly known in Kenya as the Hunter's (*Chalcomitra hunteri*). Like the scarlet-chested sunbird (*Chalcomitra senegalensis*) which can also be seen in these three parks, the Somali scarlet-chested is common throughout the bush country of Somaliland and Eastern Kenya.

Finches and waxbills, generally ground feeders, are seen in numbers. The red-billed fire finch (*Lagonosticta senegala*), a small and friendly waxbill, is usually near the lodges because of the pickings to be found there. The African fire finch (*Lagonosticta rubricata*) is more likely to be further afield, small, deep red and brown with blue-grey bill. The Jameson's fire finch (*Lagonosticta jamesoni*) has a blue-grey bill and the lovely, romantically-named purple grenadier (*Granatina ianthinogaster*) is a red-billed, cinnamon-brown waxbill with a black tail and cobalt blue rump.

The biggest of the larger birds, found mostly in the drylands back from the river, are the ostriches: the Somali or blue-shanked ostrich not found in the south, with its blue-grey neck and thighs, and the 'Maasai' ostrich which, unlike its Somali cousin, is quite common further south.

The secretary bird (*Sagittarius serpentarius*) is also large, a long-legged, crested, grey bird of prey which struts the flatlands in search of its diet of snakes and rodents, competing for them with the buzzards, hawks, goshawks and kites. The goshawks will be the African (*Accipiter tachiro*), the pale chanting (*Melierax poliopterus*) and the dark chanting (*Melierax melabates*).

The most likely eagle to be seen will be the African fish eagle (*Cuncuna vocifer*), wherever there is water, the martial (*Polemaetus bellicosus*), the slightly smaller tawny (*Aquila rapax*) and, smaller still, the long-crested hawk eagle (*Lophoaetus occipitalis*), blackish with feathered legs and distinguishing crest.

In their far and wide search for carrion, the vultures include the entirely dark-brown hooded (*Necrosyrtes monachus*); the white headed (*Trigonoceps occipitalis*) with its white crown and secondaries; the huge brown lappet-faced (*Torgos tracheliotus*) sometimes catalogued as the Nubian; the Ruppell's Griffon (*Gyps ruppellii*) and the Egyptian (*Neophron percnopterus*) small, black and white with wedge-shaped white tail.

Ground species in all three reserves include the yellow-necked spurfowl (*Pternistis leucoscepus*) — exceptionally good eating (oh, perish the thought) — the crested francolin (*Francolinus sephaena*); and the spectacular vulturine guinea-fowl (*Acryllium vulturinum*)

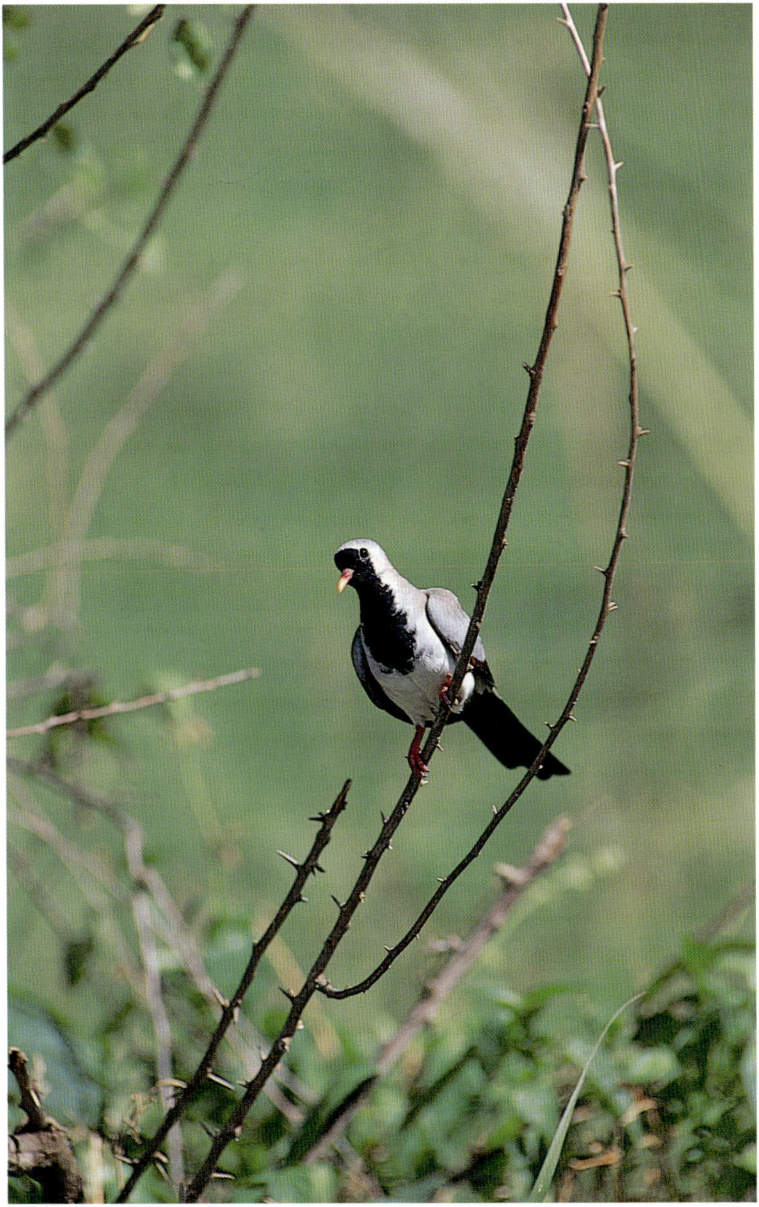

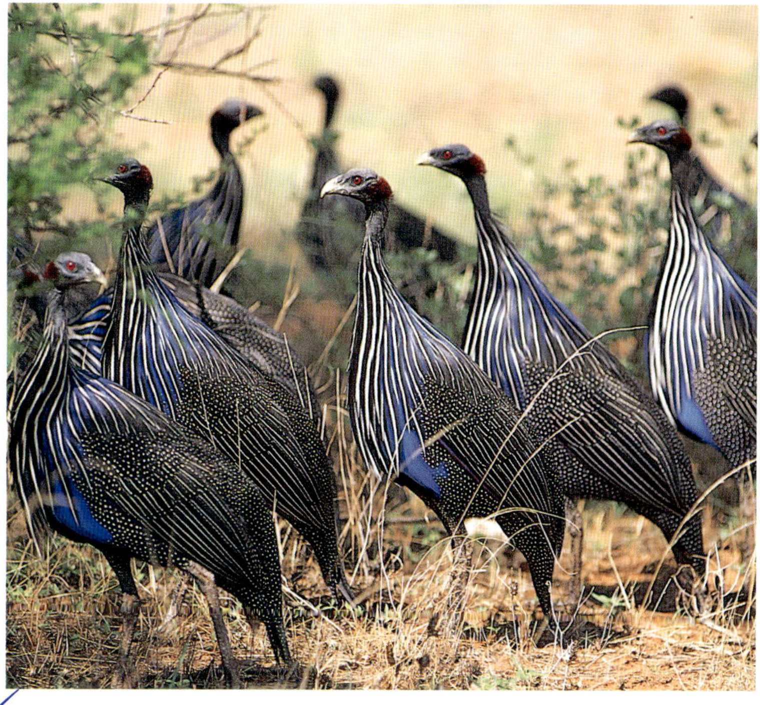

Above: Vulturine guinea-fowl (Acryllium vulturinium) *with their spectacular white, black and cobalt-blue feathered mantles are residents of the dry, thornbush country.*

Right: The Crowned crane (Balearica regulorum) *found widely in Kenya, is also the national emblem of Uganda.*

Opposite: The Namaqua dove (Oena capensis) *sparrow-sized with a long tail, is common to all three reserves in sandy and bush areas.*

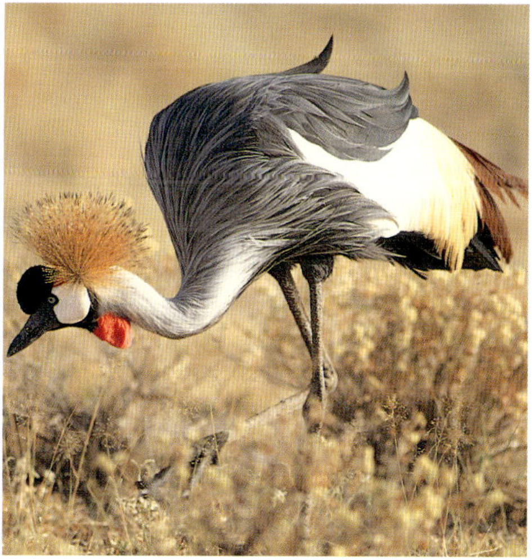

recognisable by its theatrical upper mantle feathers of striped white, black and cobalt-blue.

On the sandbanks of the Uaso Nyiro sand plover will be either the Kittlitz's (*Charadrius pecuarius*) at about sixteen-and-a-half centimetres, or the great sand plover (*Charadrius leschenaultii*), larger than the Kittlitz's by some ten centimetres.

Dry as huge areas of these three reserves may be, and although Shaba, particularly, was once a much favoured game-bird shooting area, birdlife remains prolific and rewarding and any visitor — even if only remotely interested in avifauna — is recommended to carry an illustrated guide for more comprehensive identification. Much help will be found in *The Birds of East and Central Africa* by J G Williams of which the latest and most up-dated version to the 1963 edition and reprints was published by Collins in 1992.

National interest in the beautiful birds of Kenya was confirmed with the eleven-denomination definitive postage stamp issue of February 1993, each illustrating a different species. Ten out of the eleven selected may be spotted without too much difficulty in the Samburu, Shaba and Buffalo Springs reserves. On stamp values ranging from fifty cents to Kshs 100/- they are: the superb starling; the red and yellow barbet; the greater honey guide; the malachite kingfisher; the speckled pigeon; the cinnamon-chested bee-eater; the scarlet-chested sunbird; the Reichenow's weaver; the yellow-billed hornbill and the Hadada ibis. The single exception is the lesser flamingo which illustrates the stamp of the Kshs 80/- value.

Working the Samburu, Shaba and Buffalo Springs area under extremely dry conditions during International Birdwatch 1993, two Kenya teams, each of four ornithologists, saw and positively identified eighty-two and 158 different species respectively.

Seventy-six teams competed in destinations worldwide and, within the set-time period for all of October 9-10, 1993, 797 different species were seen and recorded in Kenya.

Though admittedly some are uncommon and others rare, nearly 400 different bird species have been recorded in the three parks.

Overleaf: A useful landmark for strangers, massive 300-metre-high Lololokwe dominates the landscape for miles around.

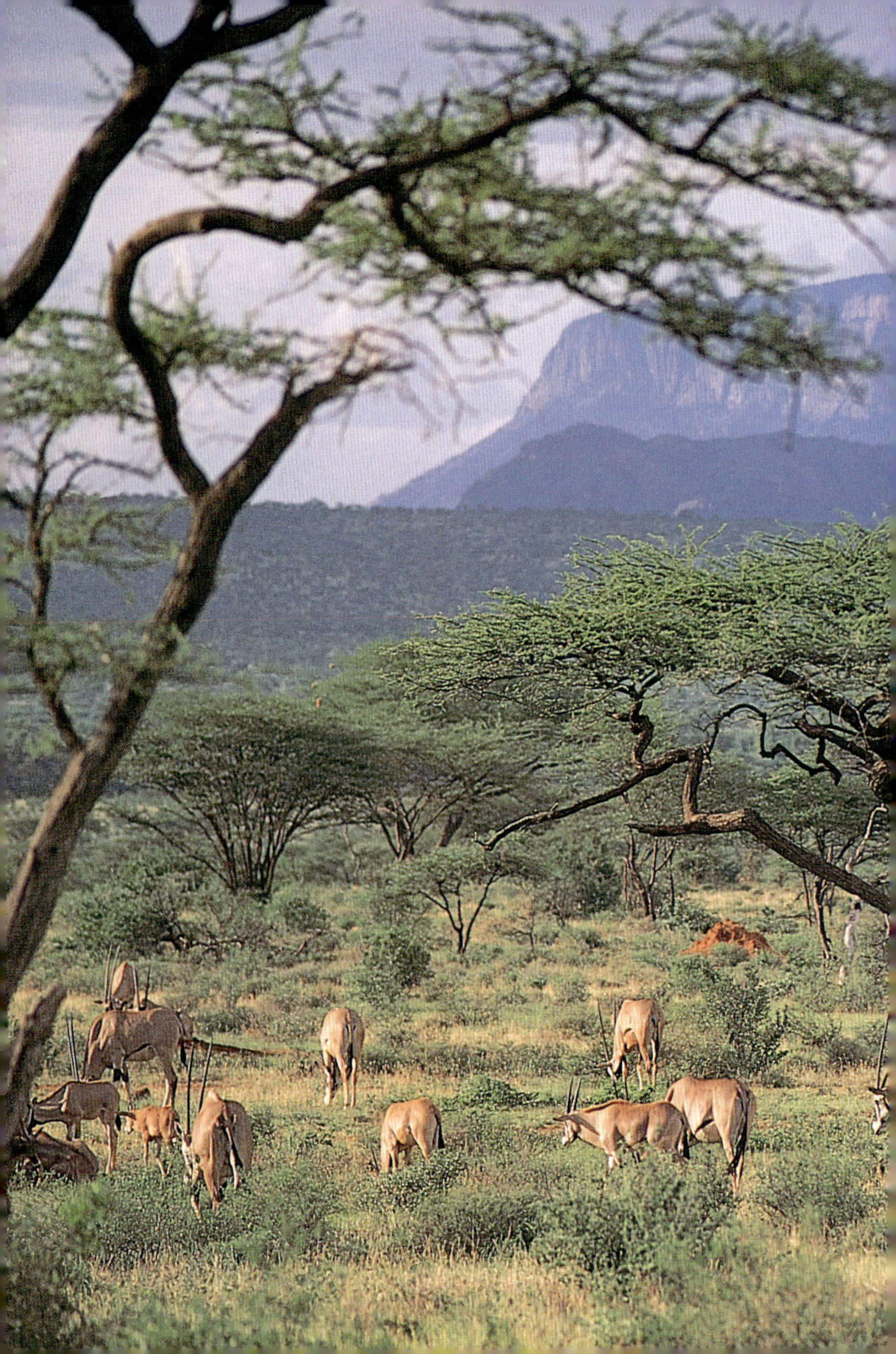

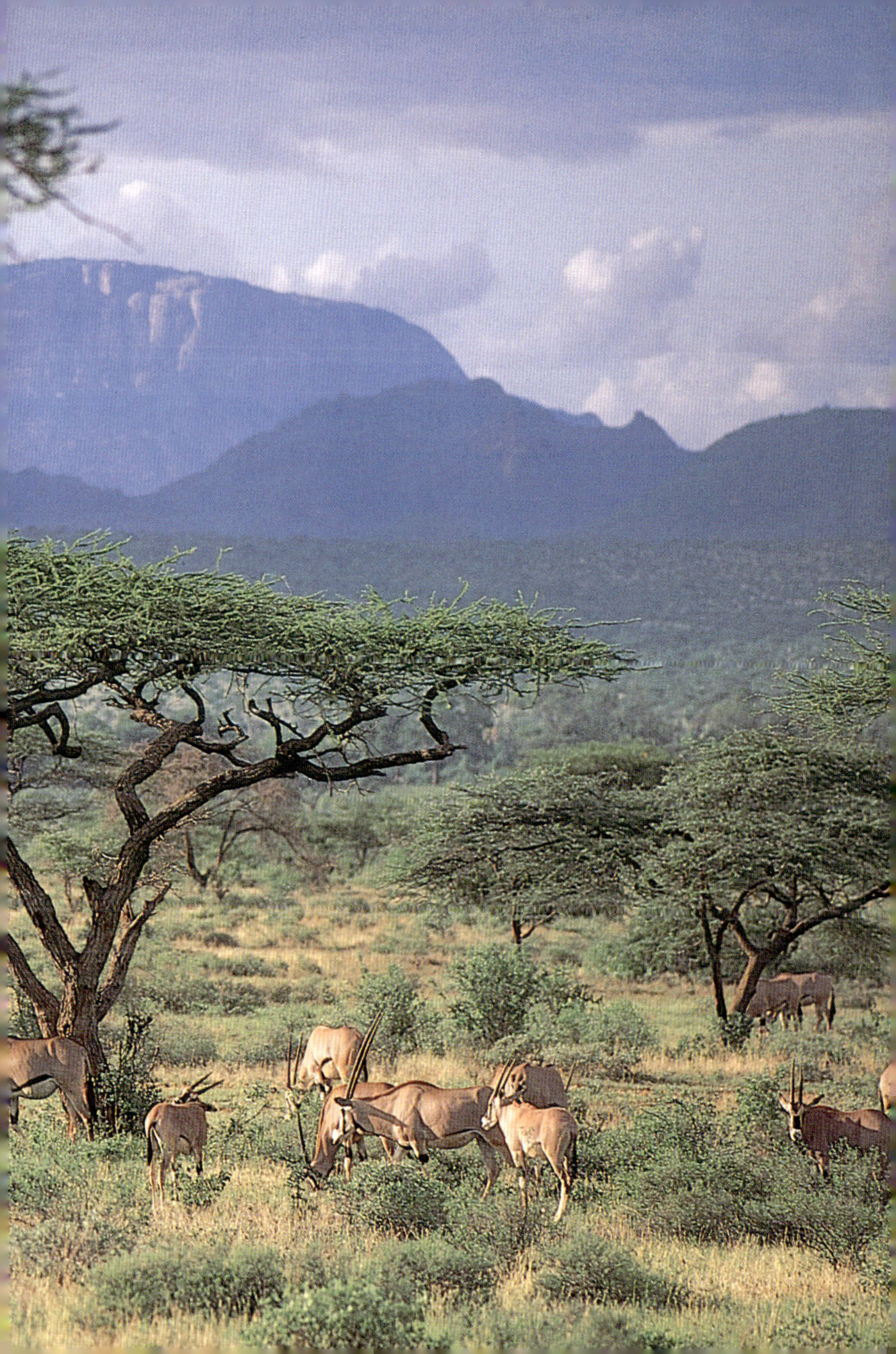

8. Accommodation

In the Samburu reserve **SAMBURU LODGE** — managed by Block Hotels, Kenya's oldest-established hotel organisation — has always been a great favourite with Kenya's residents and visitors, with its riverside gardens, shady trees, miraculous birdlife, delightful garden swimming pool (with bar) and public rooms and bedrooms all facing the river. From the 'Crocodile Bar' at riverbank level, guests can safely watch and photograph the amphibians and bait hung out in the trees across the river attracts leopards for night-time viewing and photography.

The open-fronted dining room overlooking the river ensures that no wildlife or bird-watching time is lost while eating.

Set in ten acres of natural riverine forest, accommodation comprises thirty twin and eight single rooms in thatched bungalows, all with bathroom and toilet en suite. An attractively built river-facing double-storey bedroom wing of local stone and timber contains twenty-five twin rooms and one single. All rooms have their own verandahs

The canopy of tree-shade beside the river, along which the resident ornithologist leads an hour-long bird walk twice daily (for which a small fee is payable), is a delight for keen bird people. For guests who have flown in, the lodge management will arrange game drives in the early morning and evening on either a seat-in-car or exclusive use of vehicle basis. Samburu traditional dancers perform each afternoon for which, again, a small fee is payable.

LARSEN'S CAMP, seven kilometres downstream from Samburu Lodge, is also managed by Block Hotels, a luxury tented camp where meticulous attention is paid to comfort, superior service and sophisticated cuisine.

Seventeen tents on raised timber platforms are sited on the river banks between acacia trees and doum palms. Thirteen are twin-bedded, four are tented suites, each with one double and one single bed. Each tent has flushing toilet and hot water shower en suite.

A far cry from roughing it under canvas Boy Scout style, Larsen's is richly furnished. Thickly woven Kenya carpets scatter the floors. Dinners are romantic, silver service, candlelit affairs and a devastating range of 'colonial' cocktails and liqueurs are served in the small, very personal, tented bar.

SAMBURU INTREPIDS CLUB, in the south-west sector of the reserve, is another luxury tented camp, operated by Prestige Hotels and kept small intentionally. With accommodation for a maximum of fifty guests, the keynote is a flattering personalised service.

Of imaginative layout, beneath shady riverside fig and acacia trees, the open dining room, lounge and bar are on spacious decks overlooking the water. Sleeping is in large, elegantly furnished tents under palm-thatched roofs, each with bathroom en suite (flush toilets, shower and double wash-hand basins).

The raised decks and the swimming pool in the garden are delightful places to relax. Transfers to and from the airstrip are arranged. Comfortable vehicles can be hired for game drives and, for those with more energy, camel and walking safaris are organised for exploration of the surrounding bush country.

On the opposite bank of the river, **SAMBURU SERENA** is a palm-thatched, tree-shaded permanent structure, a very much improved lodge since Samburu River Lodge pioneered development on this same site in the 1970s. All sixty-two bedrooms have bathrooms en

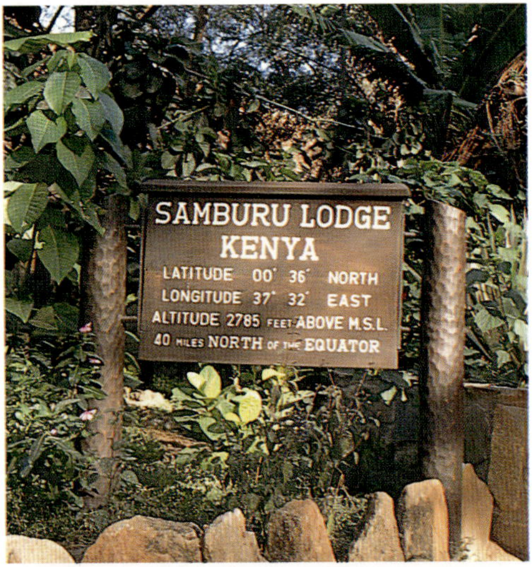

Left: Your welcome to Samburu Lodge.

Below: No time need be lost in river-watching when lunching at Samburu Serena Lodge.

Opposite: The beadwork and ornamentation which they themselves wear can be purchased — after some expected bargaining — from Samburu women at their roadside stalls outside the three reserves.

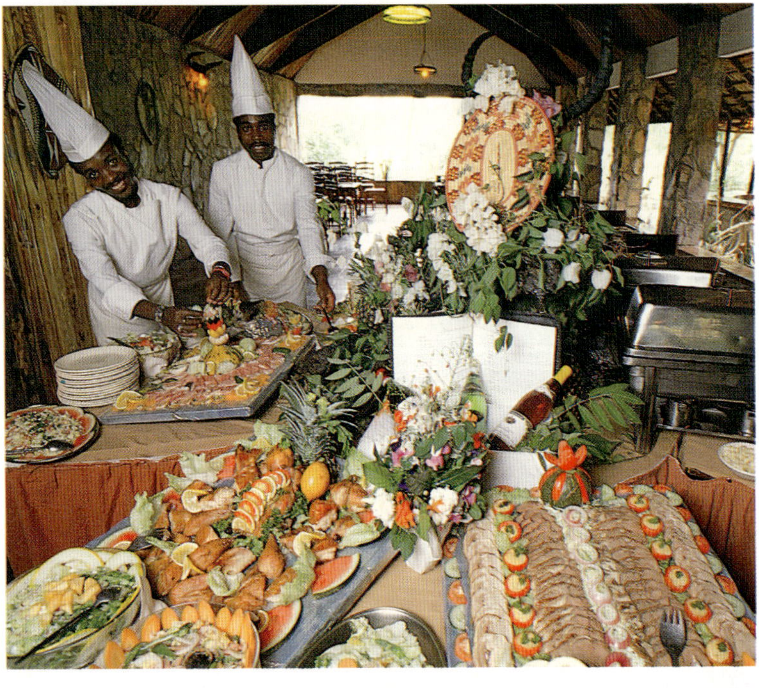

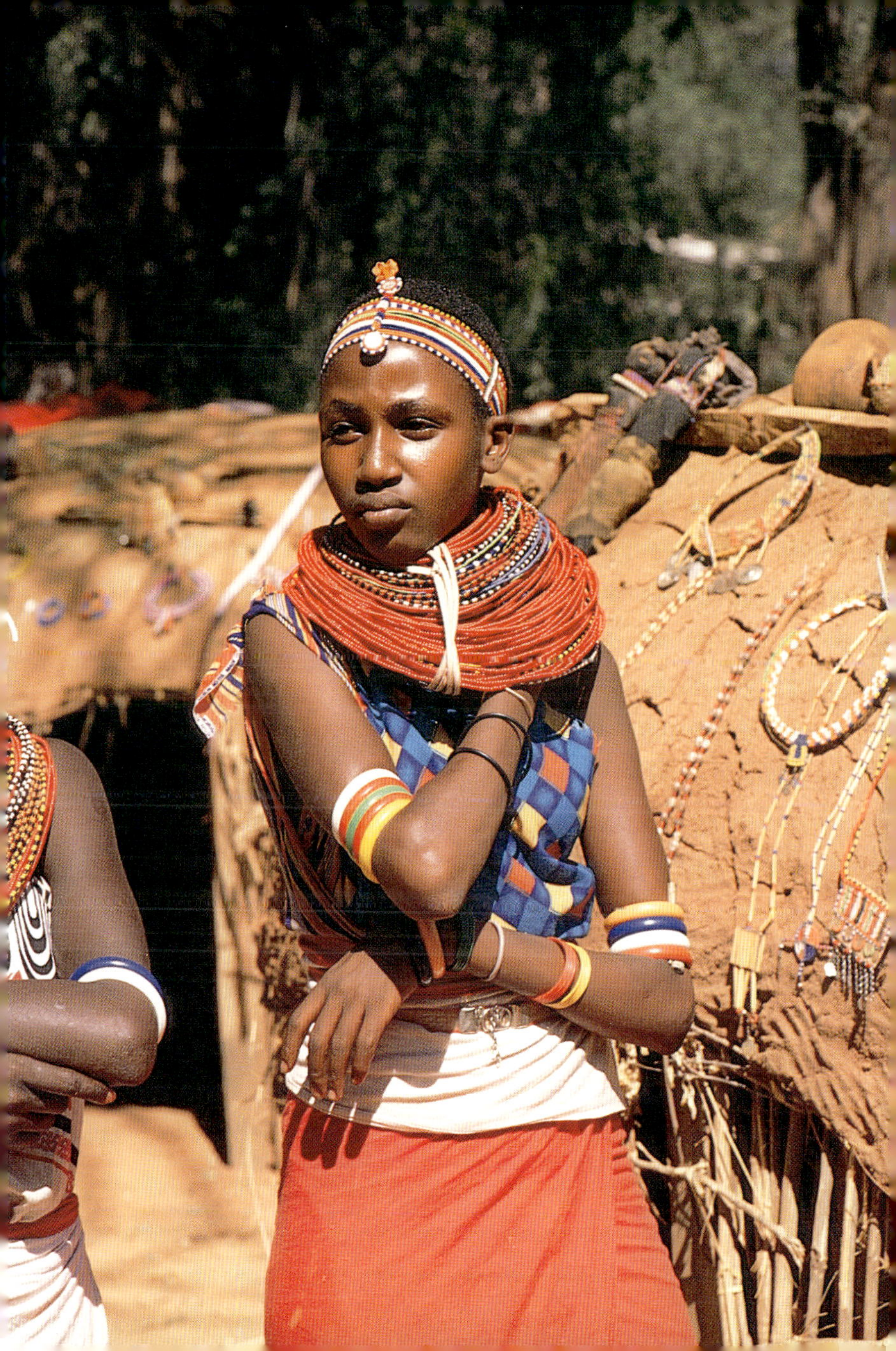

suite and a private verandah overlooking the river. Bird watching is particularly rewarding from the gardens and the large swimming pool is a delight on a typical dry-heat Samburu day. Camel safaris can be arranged.

The lodge, which maintains the high standards of comfort, service and cuisine of the several other establishments in Kenya under the Serena Lodges and Hotels flag, is situated in the north-west sector of the Buffalo Springs reserve just west of the bridge across the river. It is the lodge closest to the Buffalo Springs airstrip.

Since 1990 **BUFFALO SPRINGS LODGE** — Buffalo Springs Tented Camp as it used to be — has bed accommodation for ninety-two guests in twenty-three cottages, four bandas, seven tents and an annexe. Originally it was the only accommodation in the Buffalo Springs reserve.

In 1968, encouraged by an influx of visitors and the success of their first three self-help rondavels *Duma* (Cheetah), *Nyati* (Buffalo) and *Mamba* (Crocodile), George and Joy Adamson persuaded the Isiolo County Council to construct and administer three additional self-help bandas with cooking facilities and *Simba* (Lion), *Chui* (Leopard) and *Twiga* (Giraffe) became operational in 1974. By 1977 the volume of visitors requiring in-park accommodation had increased to such an extent that the council brought in the Kenya Tourist Development Corporation (KTDC) and African Tours & Hotels as partners to manage the accommodation and convert it into a proper tourist lodge and in 1978 Buffalo Springs Lodge Ltd was formed. Thirty tented units under picturesque *makuti* shade roofs and the timber and stone service block date back to that time.

While remaining predominantly a tented lodge for the next ten years, a major renovations programme started in 1990 saw twenty-three tents converted into permanent cottages and additional rooms created by a face-lift to the bandas and rondavels.

Located only a short distance from the springs, which have attracted thousands since the early explorers set off on foot-expeditions to the Uaso Nyiro, the dining room, lounge and bar have been a haven in the desert for passing as well as in-lodge guests, serving meals and drinks and offering the welcome chance of a cool dip.

Managed by the African Tours & Hotels group, charges are modest for accommodation and meals.

SAROVA SHABA, the only permanent accommodation in the Shaba reserve, is one of the finest in the north, of outstanding design and construction and offering very superior accommodation. Much of the stone used in the building work was quarried locally.

The site was selected originally because of the several bubbling springs which emerge there to create a natural oasis. Fast flowing rivulets have been incorporated into the layout and tumble prettily through the public rooms and patios and feed the large garden swimming pool which, surrounded by rock gardens and water plants, is illuminated at night.

The cool, spacious, timbered dining room, open on three sides, is at first-floor level above the open, ground floor, stone-paved patio and bar and commands views up, down and across the river

The eighty bedrooms in two-storey, air-conditioned blocks of four, are generously proportioned, furnished with custom-made dark woodwork. Huge walk-in mosquito nets surround the beds. Sliding picture windows on two sides invite any breeze there is and look out onto the river and the garden. All the bathrooms are en suite with quantities of hot and cold water from the taps throughout the night and day. There are four junior suites and one de luxe suite with lounge and jacuzzi — in all, 170 beds.

The lodge is owned and managed by Sarova Hotels.

The Public Camp Sites

It is essential to be entirely self-sufficient with all camping equipment, food, water, petrol and night lamps if planning to stay at the public camp sites in these three reserves. There are no facilities for purchasing anything inside the parks except at the gift shops in the permanent lodges where such items as maps, paperbacks, camera film, cosmetics and limited (non-prescription) pharmaceuticals are usually available.

Booking of the public camp sites can be done at the reserve gates.

SAMBURU — three public camp sites are situated west of Samburu Lodge, one between the Game Warden's Office and the bridge. There are also two 'special' camp sites situated just east of Samburu Intrepids Club and one just east of the reserve's West Gate between the gate and the river.

BUFFALO SPRINGS — there are no public camp sites close to the Uaso Nyiro in the Buffalo Springs reserve but six pretty sites in the park's south-eastern sector. These are the Ngare Mara Camp Sites 1, 2, 3 and 4 along Champagne Ridge, one on the Isiolo-Keromet River (the Isiolo River Camp Site) and one on the Maji ya Chumvi River (the Kubi Panya Camp Site).

SHABA — the Dakadima Camp Site is the only one near the Uaso Nyiro. Access is from the main park road (the E8lO) which links the Natorbe and the Gafarsa Gates. The pretty Funan Camp Site, practically in the centre of the park, is in the shadow of the 1,632-metre Shaba massif and close to a small green seasonal swamp. The Acacia Camp Site (yes, there are some acacia trees there) is the one closest to the Natorbe Gate.

Between them, the three reserves can truly be said to have some of the most distinguished in-park guest accommodation in Kenya. At the other end of the affordable scale, there are also some of the most pleasant, least disturbed, public camp sites from which to explore the river, springs, flatlands, hills, mountains and lonely secret places of these unforgettable golden lands.

*Overleaf: Most handsome of the giraffe species indigenous to Kenya, the Reticulated (*Giraffa reticulata*) of the north are of a much deeper chestnust colour traced with a network of white lines.*

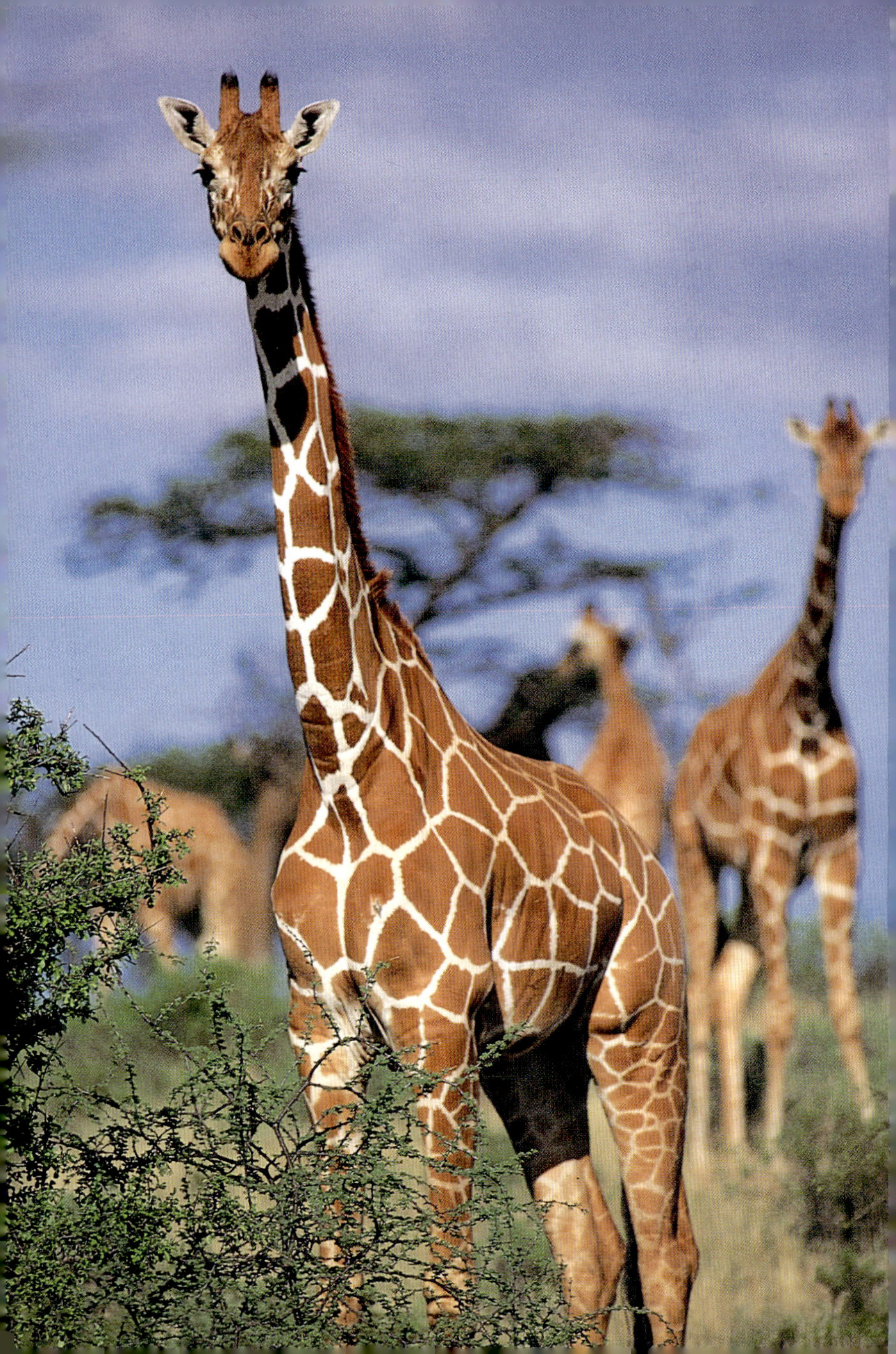